KIDS IN america

A **Gen X** Reckoning

Liz Prato

sfwp.com

Library of Congress Cataloging-in-Publication Data

Names: Prato, Liz, author.

Title: Kids in America : a Gen X reckoning / Liz Prato.

Description: Santa Fe, NM : SFWP, [2022] | Summary: "Generation X was born between the legions of Baby Boomers and Millennials, and was all but written off as cynical, sarcastic slackers. Yet, Gen X's impact on culture and society is undeniable. In her revealing and provocative essay collection, KIDS IN AMERICA: A GEN X RECKONING, Liz Prato reveals a generation deeply affected by terrorism, racial inequality, rape culture, and mental illness in an era when none of these issues were openly discussed. Examined through the lens of her high school and family, Prato reveals a small, forgotten cohort shaped as much by Sixteen Candles and Beverly Hills, 90210, as it was by the Rodney King riots and the threat of nuclear annihilation. Prato is unflinching in asking hard questions of her peers about what behavior was then acceptable or overlooked, and how we reconcile those sins today. KIDS IN AMERICA illuminates a generation that is often cited, but rarely examined beyond the gloss of nostalgia"—Provided by publisher.

Identifiers: LCCN 2021046520 (print) | LCCN 2021046521 (ebook) | ISBN 9781951631253 (trade paperback) | ISBN 9781951631260 (ebook)

Subjects: LCSH: Generation X—United States—History. | United States—Social conditions—1980- | United States—Civilization—1970- | United States—History—1969-

Classification: LCC HQ799.7 .P73 2022 (print) | LCC HQ799.7 (ebook) | DDC 305.2—dc23/eng/20211006

LC record available at https://lccn.loc.gov/2021046520

LC ebook record available at https://lccn.loc.gov/2021046521

Published by SFWP
369 Montezuma Ave. #350
Santa Fe, NM 87501
sfwp.com

Dedicated to all the friends, sisters,
and brothers
who didn't make it this far.

Table of Contents

Part I

*We are slightly overeducated
and adrift in a miasma of
social inequality.*

—Victor Chayet
Kent Denver County Day
Class of 1984

Gen X Prep

We were privileged. We were mostly white, although a few of us were Black or Hispanic or Asian or Native American. We were old money and new money and not a lot of money, but the majority of us were upper-middle class. In movies and TV shows that depicted schools like ours, the kids drove BMWs and Mercedes and Porches and Corvettes. We didn't drive BMWs and Mercedes and Porches and Corvettes. We drove brand new Jeeps and Jettas, used VW Rabbits and hand-me-down station wagons. Some of us didn't have cars, so we bummed rides from the ones who did, or from our parents.

Our school had once been two: the Kent School for girls, and Denver Country Day for boys. In 1974, they went from two schools to one, becoming Kent Denver Country Day. The school's website now says that is when our school became Kent Denver, when "Country Day" was dropped, but we know differently. KDCD was on our sweatshirts and notebooks and report cards and diplomas in the eighties. We were Kent Denver Country Day—aristocratic, plutocratic, elite—for longer than the school admits.

We didn't have cheerleaders or prom queens or homecoming kings, and we didn't take shop or auto mechanics or typing or home-ec. We took classes that would prepare us for the SATs, that would prepare us for college, that would prepare us for a career in the professions— Shakespeare and French and European history and biology and Yale and Tulane and Brandeis and Duke. We were expected to be lawyers and doctors and architects and bankers and other people who did things with money. We would own and we would sell: land, oil, stocks, coaxial cable, uranium.

Only a few of us didn't go to college or finish college because we had to work, because we needed money and were needed by family. Those of us who did make it through college graduated into a recession, and boomeranged back to our parents' houses and took jobs in coffee shops and clothing stores and gourmet markets and pubs. We tried this career, then that, and then still changed to another. We became employed and unemployed more times than we could count. We are still counting.

We were born while young men dying in faraway jungles and young people dying in nearby demonstrations and our president betraying democracy were shown on nightly TV. We were born into the hope of the moon landing and into the despair of the murders of Dr. King and Bobby Kennedy. We bounced around in the backs of station wagons without seatbelts and rode bikes without helmets. We had telephones before answering machines, and TVs before VCRs, and Dewey Decimal before Wikipedia. We watched a lot of TV. We heard new music from the radio and our older siblings and record stores where we flipped through bins and held vinyl in our hands. We watched Prince and George Michael and Michael Jackson and Joe Strummer the first time their videos were on MTV.

We celebrated the patriotism of America's bicentennial and the pride of Colorado's centennial, and we watched Kunta Kinte kidnapped and beaten and maimed by Ben Cartwright and Lou Grant and Mr. Brady. We stood in line to watch *Star Wars*, and then *The Empire Strikes Back,* and then stood in line to watch them again. We spent 444 days praying that fifty-two American hostages would be safely released from captivity in Iran. We watched the attempted assassination of Ronald Reagan and the attempted assassination of Pope John Paul II and the successful assassination of John Lennon. We cheered the U.S. men's Olympic hockey team to win the Miracle on Ice against the USSR, underscoring that the Cold War was very much alive.

We played the earliest wave of video games: Pong and Space Invaders, Asteroids and Galaxian. We lived seventy miles from The North American Aerospace Defense Command and the Cheyenne Mountain Missile Defense Center, with a bunker built to deflect a thirty-megaton nuclear explosion, and we were thirty miles from the Rocky Flats nuclear weapons plant. We watched our world turn to nuclear winter on *The Day After* in 1983.

We were called latchkey cynical lazy sarcastic flighty disaffected alienated easily-distracted late- blooming self-involved aimless apathetic skeptical pessimistic self-medicating impatient angry uncommitted won't-grow-up purposeless unreliable slackers.

We are the first generation in modern history to make less money than our parents.

We are the last generation to live without fear of being gunned down in school. We are the last generation raised without awareness of neurocognitive disorders and mental illness in kids. We are not the last generation to look the other way—or be oblivious—when those among us sexually assault those among us at parties, but we suspect—we hope—we are the last generation that figured it seemed okay for male teachers to have sex with the girls. We are the first generation to lose our virginity when sex was linked to a deadly disease—one that our president long refused to name, much less give a shit about.

We build new companies and nonprofits and technology. We write books and write code, and are doctors and teachers and lawyers; we direct plays and make music and TV shows. We manage restaurants and raise families and dance powwow and serve in the Navy. It's said we're the last generation raised without the threat of terrorism, but we lost people we loved to terrorism before 9/11, before Oklahoma City. We lost ourselves to freak accidents and addiction and mental illness and suicide and rare cancers and white supremacy. We ended up in rehab and cults and homeless shelters and bankruptcy and morgues.

We are Gen X Prep.

The Indian Way

Eight minutes and twenty seconds into the movie *Thunderheart*, FBI agents Ray Levoi and Frank "Cooch" Coutelle drive into the Badlands of South Dakota. In a cinematic trompe-l'oeil, the sun moves across the peaks and valleys, making it appear as if the camera is panning from light to dark, from dark to light. The land and the sky are pristine, blush with the beauty of the divine. The next shot zooms in on a rusty, bullet-riddled sign that has fallen to the ground, and apparently no one cares enough to fix: Entering Bear Creek Indian Reservation. In less than fifteen seconds the film telegraphs the juxtaposition of life on the reservation: natural beauty lives side-by-side with human violence and poverty.

Cooch and Ray are on the Bear Creek Reservation to investigate the murder of tribal council member, Leo Fast Elk—a case they're expected to wrap up in three days. As Cooch and Ray arrive in town, they pass simple single-story houses, children riding rusty tricycles in the street, dogs grazing on scraps, and broken-down pickups languishing in yards. "Look at this," Cooch says. "We have a third world slap-dab in the middle of America. It's hard to believe, huh?"

This would only be hard to believe if you'd been living in a gold-plated ivory tower with no access to, you know, any of the outside world. The movie was produced and set in the early 1990s, so it's not like no one—much less federal agents—knew that poverty existed in

America. For that matter, the images flashing across the screen don't depict a socioeconomic station any worse than inner city Baltimore or Detroit or South Central L.A. But the film wants us to know the Sioux Indians used to own all the land from there up into Canada, and now they're poor as shit.

Thunderheart was filmed on the Pine Ridge Reservation in South Dakota, home to the Oglala Sioux Nation. It's achingly beautiful land, where the dramatic southern Badlands transition into high-grassed prairie. It's also currently one of the poorest communities in the United States. Poverty rate statistics for Pine Ridge vary greatly depending on the source, ranging from 40% to 98%, and unemployment rates from 17.3% to 80%. Even if you take the low end of the scale (provided by the 2018 census), it's not great. Pine Ridge is often ascribed with having the youngest adult mortality rate in the U.S., although my attempts to corroborate this with reliable data resulted in a dead-end. Out of curiosity, I recently read the Spirit World section of the local paper, *Native Sun News Today*. The obituaries were sobering. Of the seventy-five people who journeyed to the spirit world in a three-month period, 61.5% were under the age of 60: Leah Ann White Bull was 48. Whisper Wind Cottier was 17. Jarelle Daniel Long Soldier was 29. Vernon Two Crow was 57. Charles Ray Badger Jr. was 36, and Waniyetu Ska Win Piper was three months and eighteen days.

The Pine Ridge reservation stretches over 2.1 million acres, only 4% of which is suitable for agriculture. It's a food desert, both literally and metaphorically. Diabetes, alcoholism, and suicide rates far exceed the national average. The weather can be harsh, with hot summers marked by sky-blackening thunderstorms and tornados, the winter a battering of snow and ice with few barriers to high winds. It's not an easy place to live, yet it is where my high school friend, Mina Stays Light, has chosen to settle.

It's hard to pinpoint exactly where Mina's story beings. Where do any of our stories truly begin? Okay, sure, she was born in 1967.

But maybe her story started nine months earlier when her unmarried teenage mother became pregnant. Maybe Mina's origin story is how she was sent to be raised by her grandparents on the Fort Berthold Indian reservation in North Dakota with the promise that her mother would retrieve Mina once she got a job and was independent. Or maybe Mina's story starts with the Mandan and the Hidatsa and the Arikara people, who hunted and farmed and fished on great expanses of prairie long before Europeans arrived, later settling in North Dakota and forming the Three Affiliated Tribes, in which Mina is enrolled. This stop-and-start search for the beginning is precisely why humans are obsessed with genealogy and psychology: we hope that if we can discover where we came from, then we will understand who we are.

The story I wanted to follow was how Mina went from attending a prep school in Denver's wealthiest neighborhood to living on an impoverished reservation. That story starts in 1979, when she was living with her mother—who had retrieved her from Fort Berthold when Mina was six—and attending public school on Denver's West Side. Mina scored so high on an aptitude test that the school administrators told her there was "this school" they wanted her to test for; she might even qualify for a scholarship. "This school" was Kent Denver Country Day, just ten miles southeast, but an entire galaxy away.

✛

Like many Euro-Americans, my family passes around a myth of Native American ancestry. A cousin recently told me that our grandfather's biological father was from a Southern Plains tribe. "That's why his skin was so dark," she said. "And he had such high cheekbones."

I was immediately wary of this assertion—not just because so many of these claims among white people are untrue, and not just because my cousin's memory has been faulty on other issues, but also because my mom, when she was still alive, told me a different story. She told me that her great aunt had been in love with a Native American man. She'd left her husband for him, and it was very scandalous. In my mom's story, no children were born of the relationship. My mom also told me that *maybe* she, herself, was 1/32 Native American, but admitted she had no proof. I regarded it as nothing more than an anecdote that had little to do with me, since I'm adopted and don't share my beloved mom's blood.

For some reason, this didn't stop me from relaying the story about my great-great aunt or my mom's possible 1/32 Native American blood to Mina and her Oglala Lakota husband when I saw them at our 20th high school reunion in 2005. It was before I knew that white people did stupid shit like this all the time, and that it was a joke—at best—among Natives. Many Euro-Americans claim they're part Native American without one iota of proof or commitment to Native communities. Sure, we want to claim the powwow and regalia and wood flutes and heart-beat drums, while also getting to opt out of the poverty and poor health outcomes and inter-generational trauma of our people being systematically killed. Ironically, in *Thunderheart*, the opposite is true: Ray is one-quarter Sioux from his biological father, but pretends his heritage is 100% Northern European. He lies that he never knew his dad when, in fact, he had watched his father drink himself to death. Ray has buried his intergenerational trauma deep.

At my 20th reunion, I was trying so hard to relate to my former classmates, to put behind the differences and cliques of high school, to form bonds between us as adults, that it didn't occur to me that saying, "Hey, my mom might have been a tiny part Indian" is not at all the same as, "You live in San Diego? I used to go there when I was a kid." It didn't occur to me that I, like white people historically have, was trying to steal something from Native Americans: their unique identity.

✛

Mina was the only Native American student at Kent Denver when she started seventh grade. She immediately bonded with Latinas who'd also come from West Side public schools, but her first year was not a good one. "The bigotry, the racism I experienced was not something I was prepared for," she said.

Not just being a minority, but also a singularity, meant Mina's ethnicity and culture was simultaneously regarded as a novelty by the administration, and completely disregarded in her day-to-day experiences at school. When her mother attended a parent-teacher night, a history teacher made mention of the "wrong" way to plant seeds: by just tossing them onto the ground, instead of fastidiously digging a hole for each one. "That's the lazy way," he said. "The Indian way." Her mother talked to the Headmaster about the teacher's offensive comments, but the teacher—and administration—didn't apologize.

Reading *Tom Sawyer* spawned its own issues. Back then, we weren't culturally aware enough to discuss the book's problematic view of Indians, and next thing you know, kids were calling Mina "Injun Joe." One student constantly crank-called her house, asking, "Injun Joe, are you home, are you home?" Mina never told any adults. "What was the point?" she said. "It would probably just make it worse. It seemed like it was just something I had to put up with."

On the flip side was the upper school Dean of Students, who knew Mina danced powwow and asked if she'd perform for the school. He saw it, I assume, as an opportunity to expose the student body to a different culture. Having already absorbed a fair amount of racism, Mina was hesitant.

"No, don't do it," one of her Latina friends cautioned her, "They're just going to make fun of you."

And Mina thought, "Yeah, you're probably right," and declined.

After interviewing Mina, I started thinking about that word—powwow—and what it meant to me when I was young. The summer camp I had attended offered sessions with three different themes: World Friendship, which surveyed global cultures and staged Olympic Games; Knighthood, which explored Arthurian legend and ended with a medieval pageant; and American Heritage, which studied life in the early American West and culminated in a powwow. During all those sessions, we sang "The Indian Song" (*Indians are high-minded, bless my soul, they're double jointed. They climb hills and don't mind it. All day long. How!*) and "We Are the Red Men" (*All of us are red men, feathers in our head men, down among the dead men, Ugh! Pow wow, pow wow*) around the campfire.

I only ever attended Knighthood, so I reached out to a woman named Deb, who had attended American Heritage, to mine her memory of the rituals. Deb said the driving force behind the powwow was a counselor named Anne, who went on to become the camp director. Anne said she was part-Native, and claimed she was teaching the kids authentic Indian traditions and dances. To the best of my knowledge there were no Native American kids or counselors at our camp, which meant that Anne got to claim Native American authority, unchecked.

Anne and her husband, Jim, presided over the powwow for decades—her in a fringed brown dress and lots of turquoise beads, and Jim crowned with a full feathered headdress. The girl campers were clad in burlap sack dresses and single feathered headdresses, while the boy campers wore loin cloths. The girls' faces and the boys' bare chests were decorated with red and yellow "war paint." While beating drums and waving feathers in the air, Anne and Jim led kids in the Buffalo Chant and the Death Dance and the Snake Dance, where sacred eagle feathers were burned. The main event of the powwow was a large boy counselor painted green (looking like a cross between the Incredible Hulk and the Jolly Green Giant, but bizarrely named "Sasquatch"), who kidnapped the Indian maidens (i.e., little girls). The boy warriors defeated him but were wounded in the process. A camper playing "medicine woman" healed them by dancing and dusting them with curative powder.

Listen, I don't have access to Anne's bloodline and can't say for certain whether she truly was or wasn't Native American. But Deb and I agreed that it's hard to believe a Native knowledgeable about her history and heritage wouldn't realize how offensive and appropriative it is for white kids to dress in burlap and loin cloths and war paint (not to mention the grown dude wearing a headdress) and hop around a campfire.

Safe to say, most white kids could have benefitted from learning about authentic powwow traditions from someone other than ill-informed, white adults. But it never should have been up to Mina, an adolescent, to be the vector of cultural education for my entire school. If someone *had* educated us, they would have described powwows as ceremonial and social gatherings that emerged in the nineteenth century to create solidarity between different Plains tribes who were forced to "migrate" off their land by the U.S. government and settle in close proximity to each other. In the early twentieth century, Wild West Shows staged powwows for white people's entertainment, boasting the exaggerated war dances that informed black and white westerns. In the 1950's, Native Americans were forced off reservations and into urban areas (the U.S. government seems to like telling them where it's okay to exist), reigniting a need for powwow as a means of connecting to each other and their culture. The powwow circuit became a thing: skilled dancers traveling across the country and competing, while traditional food and crafts were sold.

Mina started dancing powwow when she was five, while still living with her grandparents in North Dakota. In a ceremony arranged by her grandmother, Mina was given her Indian name, *Scitapathani* (which means "Little Otter"), and was bestowed with the right to wear an eagle feather. "My elders taught me a person cannot just put on an eagle feather or plume," she said. "You need to be given that right, and a prayer and song need to occur."

Mina performed Fancy Shawl Dance from ages five to thirty-one. The dance is physically demanding, involving spinning and an almost continuous crow hop. The shawl is the focus of the regalia, its draped sleeves trimmed with long fringe and ribbons. When the dancer stretches her arms, the shawl looks like butterfly wings. And like a butterfly in flight, the dance doesn't move in one straight line, but in circles and semi-circles and spirals. It moves vertical and horizontal and through planes in between.

✛

Mina's decision not to dance for the Kent Denver student body was indicative of the divide between her two lives that would continue through high school. "I didn't go to prom," she said. "I was at a powwow down in Albuquerque. That's what I wanted to do, but I also knew no one was going to ask me to prom anyway."

Mina was very pretty—with long black hair and smoky quartz eyes and a smile that anyone would be grateful to have beamed at them—and athletic, and a musician, so the assumption that no one would ask her to prom looped me for a minute. Why the hell wouldn't anyone ask her? Then it occurred to me: no one at our school ever asked *me* to prom. I was too much of the wrong things, and not enough of the right things—I talked too much, laughed too loud, sucked at sports, and didn't excel academically—and I was a white girl not on scholarship. So, if that was my reality, then it was most definitely Mina's, too.

Mina's life outside of school presented a Technicolor contrast: In powwow circles, she was considered pretty. She was a good dancer. Boys liked her (she met her now-husband at a powwow). Even though Mina didn't use this exact word, I got the sense she was popular. "So, I'd have to switch mindsets to 'Okay, here I'm nobody,'" she said about returning to school. "Here, nobody really cares."

After we graduated from Kent Denver, Mina went to Dartmouth College in New Hampshire. Dartmouth was founded in 1769 by Eleazar Wheelock, *technically* for the "education and instruction of youth of the Indian tribes. . ." except that mission was kind of bullshit. Wheelock simply used the Indian angle as a means to get donors, then quickly changed the charter to: "education and instruction for English youth and any others." From the time of Dartmouth's founding until 1970, it graduated only twenty Native American students. Only twenty *others*.

In 1970, Dartmouth's new president, John G. Kemeny, vowed to rededicate the school to its original promise of educating Native Americans. In 1972, Dartmouth launched its Native American Studies (NAS) program with one half-time professor, two classes, and fifteen recruited students. Now Dartmouth offers a major and a minor in NAS, with twenty Native-centered courses, including history, literature and poetry, law, sports, and environmental issues. When the program celebrated its fortieth anniversary in 2012, seven hundred Native Americans had graduated from Dartmouth (which is, you know, significantly better than the twenty students in its first 200 hundred years).

Mina going to Dartmouth—with financial assistance and some scholarship money from the Three Affiliated Tribes—seemed predestined. The only problem was, she couldn't afford to return after her first year. Tuition, room, and board was over $16,000. Her mother had already taken out a second mortgage on their house to help with Kent Denver, and the tribe's funds were limited. Mina had spent six years at Kent being funneled towards a prestigious college. What was she supposed to do now?

She joined the Army. Military veterans are held in high regard in Native culture, and Mina said she needed the discipline. She also admitted she'd always liked wearing a uniform. When she was a little kid in the Bluebirds, her favorite day was when they got to wear their matching blue skirts and red vests to school. "I felt like I was with a group of people," she said. "I finally fit in."

The Army instantly recognized leadership skills in Mina and chose her as First Squad Leader during basic. It meant she had to do things first; she had to be an example. But it wasn't the same kind of first like she was at Kent Denver: the first "example," the rare Native American who had to stand in for *all* Native Americans: to counteract racial stereotypes, to be the first/only Native American on the cross-country team, to be the first to play flute in band, or whatever else she was singled out for. She was not tokenized or outcast. No, the Army gave Mina authority because she was smart and fast and strong.

After getting out of the Army, Mina returned to Denver. She tried going to college on her G.I. Bill several times, but something always got in the way: getting married, having two daughters, financial responsibilities. Mina became a project manager at a telecom company, where she felt like she had to work harder than everyone else—to make up for not being a college graduate, and to counteract workplace stereotypes about Native Americans. "That was always hanging over my head," she said.

One weekend during Mina's tenure at the telecom company, she was at a Denver powwow, standing in line for the Grand Entry. Grand Entry is like the Parade of Nations for the Olympics, except way more sacred. The land is blessed, and an elder leads participants into the arena to a baritone drum beat. Mina was waiting to enter the arena from the east. She was wearing regalia for Jingle Dance, which she started dancing when she was thirty-one. A Jingle Dress, also known as a Prayer Dress, is made from rows of metal cones called *ziibaaska'iganan* sewn to buckskin or another animal hide. The dancers move in small, rhythmic steps with their hands on their hips or while waving a feather fan. The *ziibaaska'iganan* jingle against each other, evoking the sound of rain.

So, Mina was standing in line, waiting to enter the realm that had been blessed by her elders, when her dance purse vibrated. When she told me this, I thought it was some spiritual vibration and got the chills. But, no—it was her cellphone. Specifically, it was her work cellphone, contacting her on a weekend. In the past, she'd had difficulties getting time off from work to attend out-of-town powwows and other religious and cultural ceremonies. Sometimes she'd have to drive all night to get back in time for work on Monday because her employer wouldn't give her the day off. And now, she couldn't even enjoy this powwow without her job interfering. Mina realized she was over it—city life, everything that Denver stood for, working her ass off to put money in some CEO's pockets, and the split between her two lives. She wanted to completely inhabit herself and also be of use to her community.

"It wasn't like a conscious decision," Mina said. "It was more of this innate need to make things better, to make people better."

So, she quit her job at the telecom company and, with her husband and youngest daughter, moved to the Pine Ridge Reservation where her husband was raised.

✛

Pine Ridge is home to the Oglala Lakota (also known as Oglala Sioux). Per the Fort Laramie Treaty of 1868, the Great Sioux Nation also once included the Black Hills and what the U.S. calls Mount Rushmore. But as soon as settler colonists realized there was gold in them thar hills—about five years after the Laramie Treaty—the U.S. said, "Fuck it, we're taking it back," and went about settling and mining as if that whole treaty thing had never happened. The Lakota refused to cede the land, which led to the Great Sioux War in 1876. That's when the Battle of Little Bighorn and Custer's Last Stand went down, which—spoiler alert—did not go well for the U.S. The Sioux soundly defeated the Cavalry.

The U.S. Congress enacted what's known as the Sell or Starve Act, which basically said, "Give us the land or we'll cut off all aid to you."

By "aid," they meant food and water sources. To prove how serious they were, they slaughtered hordes of bison—the Plains Indians' staple food. Bit by bit, the Lakota people surrendered, which meant being pushed south onto what is now the Pine Ridge Reservation.

Pine Ridge is the primary reason I recently re-watched *Thunderheart*. My original plan had been to visit Mina on the reservation in the summer of 2020. I'd applied for a travel grant in February so I could go to South Dakota and feel the land and the air and the history. I knew where Mina had come from, and I wanted to see where she'd gone to. But by April 2020, the world was locked down due to the COVID-19 pandemic, and it was clear that I wasn't traveling anywhere in the next few months (much less onto an Indian reservation where medical resources are scarce and white people have a nasty habit of spreading deadly diseases). I remembered that *Thunderheart* had been filmed on Pine Ridge, so I downloaded it onto my iPad to at least see the land.

I recalled liking *Thunderheart* when it first came out in 1992, but was still prepared to be appalled by the appropriation of Native stories when I re-watched it in 2020. I was surprised to discover that the movie actually tells essential stories about Native history—so many, in fact, that it's pretty convoluted. A still frame at the beginning of *Thunderheart* reads, "This story was inspired by events that took place on several Indian reservations during the 1970s."

Cooch and Ray arrive during the dying days of a civil war, as the feds put it, between pro-government factions and traditionals. The "pro-government" group includes the modern tribal council, which has good relations with the United States government—perhaps to an Uncle Tom-like degree. The traditionals are Indians who want to retrieve the land, culture, and way of life ripped from them by the U.S. government.

But "who's on what side" is even more complicated than all that, because—in real life and in the movie—each side is aligned with a more militant group. In *Thunderheart*, the tribal council president is Jack Milton, whose real-life counterpart, Dick Wilson, was accused of nepotism, accepting kickbacks from companies secretly drilling for uranium, and enforcing his will through a violent militia called GOONS (Guardians of the Oglala Nation). In the movie, the traditionals are aligned with the radical Aboriginal Rights Movement (ARM), whose real-life counterpart was the American Indian Movement (AIM). After a failed attempt at impeaching Wilson in 1973 (we're still in real-life now—stay with me), AIM occupied the town of Wounded Knee for seventy-one days. This occupation is never directly discussed–and barely alluded to, really—in *Thunderheart*, but the after effects are: in the three years following the occupation, more than sixty of Wilson/Milton's opponents were mysteriously murdered, as well as at least two federal agents.

If this all seems confusing and messy, it's because it is—although in a very well-intentioned way. *Thunderheart*'s filmmaker, Michael Apted, tried to compress, fictionalize, and modernize over a hundred years of history into a two-hour movie, while also adding a personal storyline for Ray. I've now seen the movie five or six times, and only came close to understanding what was going on after I did a *lot* of independent research about the history of Wounded Knee.

Wounded Knee memorial, where AIM staged its occupation, is in south-central Pine Ridge, about twenty miles from the Nebraska border. This is where Ray has a vision of himself as one of the Native Americans massacred by the U.S. military in 1890. This slaughter is only one of many ugly, brutal acts waged against the original keepers of the land across the U.S., but Wounded Knee defines Pine Ridge.

In the late nineteenth century, Native Americans were still unhappy about the U.S. disregarding the Fort Laramie Treaty, stealing their land, starving and killing their people, and forcing them onto mostly unfertile land (go figure). Then an elder had a vision of a messiah promising that the next spring, the earth would be made anew. Water, grass, trees, buffalo, and wild horses would return, and the white man would be gone. Ancestors who had been killed would return to live among their family. In order to bring about this renewal, the people would need to perform the "Ghost Dance" envisioned by the messiah.

Ghost Dance is the very first scene of *Thunderheart*. It's never identified as such, and the words "ghost dance" are only said once, one hour and twenty-seven minutes into the movie. The film begins at night with a crescent moon hanging in the sky. We see the shadows of winter-bare trees and men with single-feathered headdresses dancing slowly. Some hold long, thin peace pipes to the sky, others wave feathers. They chant while a single drum beats and a wood flute sings. It is peaceful, sacred, a prayer. As the rising sun radiates along the horizon, the men come into clearer view. They are wearing fringed buckskin shirts, shuffling clockwise around one bare tree. They pray for hours, from dark to light. The sun climbs higher, revealing striations in the mesas and canyons, and the men dissolve until there is nothing but earth and sky. Even for the viewer uninformed about history, we know this is storied land inhabited by a deep spiritual memory.

That's the real inciting incident for *Thunderheart*—not the murder of Leo Fast Elk, not the "civil war," but the Ghost Dancers: what made them dance in the first place, how white settler colonists reacted, and every oppression and rebellion since. Because in real life, white people got totally freaked out by ghost dancing. "Indians are dancing in the snow and are wild and crazy," a white agent wrote to Washington, D.C. in November 1890. "We need protections and we need it now!" White people assumed the ghost dance was satanic. They thought it was a prelude to a massive attack. They thought this "Indian problem" had gone far enough.

Washington sent Dr. Valentine McGillycuddy, who used to be an agent on the reservation, to check things out (white agents were required to live on all Indian lands to make sure the Indians were behaving). McGillycuddy saw no real problem with the ghost dance. "If the Seventh Day Adventists prepare their ascension robes for the second coming of the Savior, the United States Army is not put in motion to prevent them. Why should not the Indians have the same privilege?"

Well, that was *not* the response Washington wanted, so they decided to arrest Sitting Bull instead. On December 15, 1890, forty-three Native American police officers surrounded the revered Lakota chief's cabin at Standing Rock. He was willing to go peacefully(-ish), but his villagers were agitated. Some started to ghost dance. One, named Catch-the-Bear, pulled out a rifle and shot at the officer trying to take away Sitting Bull. The officer shot back, accidentally hitting Sitting Bull, while another officer purposefully put a bullet in Sitting Bull's head.

Understanding that it's *really bad* when someone assassinates your leader at point-blank range, the two hundred Standing Rock residents high-tailed it out of there. They met up with Chief Spotted Elk at the Cheyenne River Reservation, who led them and some of his people to Pine Ridge to seek shelter. But they were intercepted by the 7th Cavalry, who forced them to *Cankpe Opi Wakpala*—what we call Wounded Knee Creek. At Wounded Knee, 500 Cavalry troopers surrounded the 350 Lakota people and installed four Hotchkiss guns in the hills. Hotchkiss were early machine guns capable of propelling an explosive shell for two miles, at a rate of one per-second. The guns' sights were trained so that they could mow down all the Lakota tents in a matter of minutes.

On the morning of December 29th, the Cavalry moved in to disarm the Lakota of all weapons. One named Black Coyote, who was deaf and may or may not have understood, wouldn't give up his Winchester. The soldiers tried to seize the rifle, and it discharged into the sky. The troopers lost their shit and started firing at everyone nearby. They fired at close range. They fired into tipis. They hunted down women and children who were hiding in nearby ravines. The troops pursued Native Americans on horseback for miles—not to capture them, but to kill them. At least 153 Sioux were murdered in less than an hour. Many more later died of their wounds and froze as they lay in the snow. It's estimated that nearly 300 of the original 350 Lakota were killed at Wounded Knee.

The U.S.'s slaughter of the Natives at Wounded Knee was the real inciting incident for *Thunderheart*, and a massive, intergenerational wound is what birthed—and was born from—the Ghost Dance.

✝

Mina's husband is the Service Manager for the Wounded Knee district on Pine Ridge. Residents come to his office when they need information or assistance, which Mina says "includes help turning on their propane in the winter, sealing their windows, mowing lawns, moving furniture and digging graves … whatever the needs are for the people." When I interviewed Mina in early May 2020, the list had also come to include helping people get COVID-19 emergency utility assistance and apply to be contact tracers. After moving to Pine Ridge, Mina completed her bachelor's degree at the Oglala Lakota College and is now the director of a satellite campus. "When we moved here, I decided I'm going to finish what I wanted to do," she said. "This was my time."

In this community with high poverty and unemployment, Mina and her husband are gainfully employed. The reasons for the high unemployment are complex, she said. Jobs on the reservation exist, but sometimes people can't find childcare, or they don't have reliable transportation—all conditions of poverty that perpetuate the cycle throughout the country. Sometimes people can't pass the drug test, Mina said, and sometimes, "They get their first paycheck … to them it's like they hit the jackpot." They've existed for so long in a poverty way of thinking that "they don't know what to do with it. They think it's going to last forever, and they don't go back to work."

But Mina had grown up in a big city with a working mother. She'd gone to prep school and an Ivy League college with people of privilege.

She'd been in the Army and worked as a project manager for a telecom company. She had lived experiences outside of poverty that allowed her to circumvent the cycle in which many people on the reservation get stuck.

Mina's only regret about moving to the reservation is how hard it was on her youngest daughter, who was just entering ninth grade. Because she had grown up in the city, she was seen as *other*. Mina could relate. "I told her, honestly, throughout life, I don't think anyone feels like they fit in anywhere," Mina said. But she also told me, "Living on Pine Ridge makes sense to me. Things feel as they should be."

Mina now dances Traditional Dance. Her buckskin dress is covered by a red beaded cape that she crafted by hand with her husband. Her long breastplate is made of ivory-colored imitation bone. Her dress and breastplate are embroidered with yellow stars and dragonflies in a pattern designed by her sister-in-law. Underneath Mina's breastplate is a belt, which includes a small purse and a knife holder and an awl holder—items that the women of long ago carried while they cared for their homes. The knife was used to skin animals and cut meat, the awl was for sewing, and the purse held items such as flint and bone needles. Mina's knife, carved from buffalo bone, was given to her by a female Lakota veteran when she moved to Pine Ridge. Beaded hair ties crafted by a now-deceased niece drape over Mina's shoulders. Her red moccasins were made by Millie Black Bear, an elder and traditional dancer who Mina looks up to. Every piece of Mina's regalia has meaning.

What was the meaning of the burlap sacks, the single-feathered headdresses, and the war paint worn by white kids dancing powwow at my summer camp? I'd like to say there was no meaning at all. We all played cowboys and Indians as children, we all watched grainy westerns that depicted Native Americans hopping around a campfire, we wore replicas of sacred regalia for Halloween. It was all in good fun. But there *was* meaning behind what we did: the belief that we had a right to plunder the land and culture and customs of those who came before us.

Because we had also been taught that Columbus was a hero for discovering America (not that he brought slavery and disease to the people who'd lived there for thousands of years). We learned that the Natives were helpful and generous to settlers—until they weren't, and became savage and needed to be tamed. Imbedded in grainy Saturday afternoon westerns were tales of Indians scalping whites. We ate Lands O Lakes Butter and Sue Bee Honey with "Indian maidens" as logos and hoped one day to buy a Jeep Cherokee. We wore wide-grinning Chief Wahoo on our Cleveland baseball caps, and tomahawk-chopped for the Atlanta Braves. So, while my fellow campers and I sang songs and forged new friendships and slept on ground that once belonged to the Arapaho, we did what white people have always done: we stole traditions from indigenous people, distorted them while pretending we weren't, and convinced ourselves that it was our own American heritage.

Reckoning

"**E**very white kid who went to prep school in the eighties is having a reckoning," Martin said a week after the 2018 Supreme Court confirmation hearings for Brett Kavanaugh. Martin and I talk on the phone every couple of months to deconstruct a current issue, a TV show, our jobs, our youth. During this call, our topic was Christine Blasey Ford testifying that Brett Kavanaugh had sexually assaulted her at a party in 1982.

Ford and Kavanaugh had both attended D.C. area prep schools—hers an all-girls school, his all-boys. Their schools mingled frequently. Ford knew Kavanaugh from around. The prep school Martin and I attended, Kent Denver Country Day, was co-ed, so we all mingled daily. We were always around. Ford testified to the Senate Judiciary Committee of the 115th Congress that one day after summer swim practice in 1982, she attended a small gathering at a private home, teenagers drinking in the living room. That was nearly every weekend when I was in high school—someone's parents were always out of town. There was always a living room, a keg, a garage, a backyard, a basement, a bedroom.

Ford testified that she went upstairs to use the bathroom and was suddenly shoved into a bedroom. Brett Kavanaugh and another boy came in and locked the door behind them. They turned the music up loud. Ford was pushed onto the bed and Kavanaugh climbed on top of her. He began groping her and grinding into her. He was trying to pull off her clothes, but was drunk and had a hard time negotiating the one-piece bathing suit Ford was wearing.

"I believed he was going to rape me," Ford testified. "I tried to yell for help. When I did, Brett put his hand over my mouth to stop me from screaming. This was what terrified me the most, and has had the most lasting impact on my life."

She couldn't breathe. She thought she was going to die.

The first prep school rape I heard about came through the whisper network. It was 1982, and I was Assistant to the Director for our school musical. I was a sophomore who laughed too loud and wore mannish hats and had little discernable talent in academics, the arts, or athletics. Most of the cast were juniors and seniors who were prettier and more popular than me. One day, one of those senior girls whispered to a few of us other girls: *Carl raped Sophia.*

Sophia was her best friend—beautiful, confident, and talented. I knew who Carl was but didn't know him personally. He wasn't a theater kind of guy. He didn't have to be. He was insanely rich and lacked parental supervision in a way I thought only happened in debaucherous teen movies set in Manhattan or L.A. At Carl's parties—intimate gatherings, not come one, come all keggers—the girls usually outnumbered the boys. There was Dom Perignon and crystal flutes and servants to clean up the mess. That's what I already knew about Carl. I didn't need to know anything else once I heard the whisper: *Carl raped Sophia.*

In January 2012—nearly thirty years after Carl raped Sophia—a Kent Denver student told school administrators that a friend of his had been sexually assaulted at a New Year's Eve party in Vail. The school told the sixteen-year-old girl's parents, who then notified the Vail Police Department, who then launched an inquiry. Celebrating New Year's Eve in the swanky resort town of Vail is a Kent Denver tradition. Enough kids have parents who own condos or houses in Vail (or are willing to shell out the bucks for a hotel room) that a large posse goes up and parties at those condos and houses and hotel rooms. Parents considered Vail a safe alternative to their kids driving from party to party in Denver, navigating the icy streets with the other New Year's drunks. In Vail, they'd park their car once and walk to the parties, then have a safe place to sleep. I never did New Year's Eve at Vail because that crowd—the so-called "popular" crowd—was not my posse.

The 2012 investigation into the New Year's Eve sexual assault centered on three junior boys and one sophomore girl from Kent Denver. Because they were all minors, their identities were kept anonymous. The girl gave extensive testimony to Vail detectives—only a tiny fraction of which was published by Denver media—outlining how she had agreed to meet up with the boys at the hot tub at the Arrabelle Hotel.

The Arrabelle is a borderline-fantasy resort meant to invoke the "old world, European charm" of Alpine towns—which translates into looking like an elaborate gingerbread village threw up. The Arrabelle's standard hotel rooms start at around $900 per night, with an additional twenty-six residences of one to three bedrooms, the nightly prices of which skyrocket towards $5,000. The hot tub sits on the roof of the Arrabelle. The resort's web photo gallery features a man standing in the hot tub, naked from the waist up, talking to a woman perched on its flat, square edge. It's daytime and she's still in her ski clothes, with her pants pushed up to her knee, her boots on the ground, and one bare foot dangling in the water. The narrative suggests that she's just come off the shimmering slopes rising in the background and is warming up with the hot water and hot man.

A Denver news station said they obtained "hundreds of pages of police reports, photos, text messages, videos, and documents" related to the case of the three boys and one girl, that they boiled down to a 1,942-word article. That's all the information I have at my disposal: the 1,942 words that CBS4 Denver chose to highlight. What *they* decided was important.

It said the sixteen-year-old girl told Vail Police that when she arrived at the Arrabelle hot tub, the three boys were already naked. She got in with them because she was cold (at 9:00 p.m. it was nineteen degrees, and by midnight down to twelve). She took off her shirt—but initially not her bra—and said the boys tried to help her out of her pants. She said she didn't want them touching her, so she took them off herself. They egged her on to take off her bra. Without having the exact transcript, I can nonetheless reconstruct the familiar patter. I bet most women can. One teen girl alone with three older guys cajoling, "Come on! Why not? It's no big deal. It'll be fun! What are you, chicken? Be like us. Don't you want us to like you?"

"I was just scared," she told the police. "I wanted to get out of there … if I didn't get out of there now, things were kind of going to go south with these guys."

The girl got out of the hot tub. She managed to grab a towel and her jacket and went into the hotel hallway. But she didn't have her clothes. She needed her clothes.

The term "date rape" didn't enter the public lexicon until 1985, when *Ms. Magazine* published the results of a three-year study into rape on college campuses. The study surveyed 7,000 students at thirty-five colleges, and shattered the conventional wisdom that most rapes were committed by strangers. The report revealed that one-in-four college women had experienced rape or attempted rape, according to its legal definition. However, only 25% of those women identified their experience as rape. Why? Because the perpetrator was someone they knew. Because they'd been drinking. Because she wanted to kiss him at first. Because she went into the bedroom with him. Because she had gone on one—or two or four or eight—dates with the guy. Because he didn't hit her or threaten her with a gun or a knife.

In 1982, we didn't have the terms "date rape" or "acquaintance rape." When Sophia's best friend told me and a few other girls that Carl had raped Sophia during one of his intimate parties, not a single one of us asked for clarification. There were no "What exactly …?" or "But didn't she …?" questions. Somehow, even in our protected ivory tower, we knew rape was rape. We also knew that telling anyone in power would only make it worse.

This is the part where I can't write a relevant story because it was told to me in confidence. I can say it was told to me right after the Kavanaugh hearings, when my friend Dara messaged me about being raped at a party in high school when she was too drunk to resist or give consent. If I had a right to tell her story, this is the part where I'd reveal the details:

and when Dara tried to scream for help, he put his hand over her mouth.

The last time I saw Sophia was at a party in 2015. She was just as beautiful and smart as I remembered, now a respected professional and the mother of two strong young women. We joked about the same guys we—and our friends—had kissed in high school. It was fun, it was banter, and there definitely was no mention of Carl. When the #metoo movement exploded into the public consciousness in 2017 and women enumerated the sexual assaults and rapes they had endured, I thought of the long-ago whisper about Carl raping Sophia. Could a memory stored for so long be accurate? More importantly, was it true? There was only one way to know. I asked Sophia if I could talk to her—if I could interview her—about what happened. She said yes, as long as I used a pseudonym—not out of shame, but out of caution. I'd already planned it that way. Even thirty-five years later, we both knew we needed to protect ourselves from powerful men.

Sophia and Carl dated in the fall of 1982 and slept together a few times, consensually. A couple of months into their relationship, Carl hosted a small party at his house. Just a few people—a couple other guys, a couple other girls. Everyone got hammered. Sophia remembers being really drunk, and then she remembers waking up in Carl's bedroom with him on top of her and his dick in her mouth. She couldn't speak and she couldn't breathe. She felt like she was suffocating.

Sophia managed to push Carl off her. He dressed and left the room, and someone else drove Sophia home. They broke up, and she started dating Jeremiah—a friend of Carl's who'd also been at the party that night. Sophia told Jeremiah about Carl assaulting her when she was passed out. He seemed sympathetic, she said, but also made it clear he was going to stay friends with Carl. It made Sophia think she must have been responsible for what happened to her. Because she was drunk. Because they'd already slept together. Because he didn't hit her or threaten her with a gun or a knife. She decided it was best to "suck it up" and never talk about it again. Sophia didn't even tell her husband of thirty years until the night before I interviewed her.

What haunted me most was Sophia saying more than once, "He'd always been so sweet to me." Despite the crazy hedonism I'd seen from the outside, Carl had actually been kind and gentle and treated Sophia well. Until he didn't.

On New Year's Eve in Vail, the sixteen-year-old girl was standing half-naked in a hotel hallway, and decided to go back to the hot tub to retrieve her clothes. One of the boys took her to a towel room and informed her she couldn't have her clothes unless she gave him a blow job.

"I was like, if I just cooperated … [he] would come back with my clothes," she told the police, "and then I could leave."

Just cooperate, women have heard so many times. *Don't be such a drag. Just go along with it. Why are you fighting this?*

After his blow job on-demand was completed, the boy still wouldn't return her clothes. The girl returned to the Arrabelle hallway and found her best friend. They stood in front of the elevators, trying to figure out what to do. Her friend convinced her to go back for her clothes, certain one of the boys would step up, would be *decent*, and give them to her. So, the girl returned to the hot tub again.

When the police asked why she didn't take that opportunity to leave, the girl said it's because she was half-naked and couldn't go outside. Remember, it was twelve degrees outside. Her only other option was to knock on random hotel room doors, and hope that whoever answered would see this mostly-naked teenage girl as someone to help. Maybe it sounds like an obvious choice compared to the alternative, but it doesn't take into account the humiliation a girl this age is bound to feel when half-naked and violated. It doesn't account for how trauma trumps logic.

That confusion is a common by-product of acquaintance rape— and one reason why only 25% of respondents in the *Ms. Magazine* study considered their rape to be rape. Victims are often left wondering if what happened really happened. They tell themselves maybe they're overreacting and it really wasn't that bad. They assume they *couldn't* have just been assaulted by someone who walks the same halls as them every day in their small private school.

I wonder about her friend in that hallway with her. Did she give the girl an extra item of clothing to cover up with? Did she offer to knock on doors for her? Why didn't she go with her—or *for* her—to get her clothes back? I can only guess, because all I have is the 1,942 words that CBS4 Denver decided to report. I also have intuition predicated on the experience of once having been a sixteen-year-old girl. It's possible the friend, herself, was scared of being assaulted by the boys. Or she was scared of the damage to her reputation if she stood up to them; she'd be seen as a buzzkill, a narc. Maybe she was also confused how this could have happened with guys she'd previously thought of as nice. Maybe— and I hate this possibility the most—she didn't believe her friend. Because that's what the patriarchy has trained us to do: believe men, at all costs.

So, the sixteen-year-old girl returned to the roof. She said the boys cornered her in the towel room. One told her, "You are *not* leaving right now," and the two remaining boys pressured her into giving them oral sex. Then, and only then, was she allowed to have her clothes.

Women had forgotten—or blocked or minimized—so many of the sexual transgressions made against us. Then came the 2016 election, where talk of Trump's forced kissing and pussy grabbing was daily prattle. The next fall, Harvey Weinstein was publicly outed as a serial rapist, and the #metoo movement took on full force. And the following fall, Christine Blasey Ford testified about Brett Kavanaugh assaulting her at a party. It was all so bright, so loud, so piercing. Three powerful men. Three falls in a row.

Well, this happened, was the memory tickertape I played for my husband again and again, that so many women played for each other. *And then this happened. Oh, and then there was that other time . . .*

I knew Toby from summer camp. He was a couple of years older, and I think I'd once had a crush on him. The summer I was sixteen, he was in Denver visiting his aunt and suggested we hang out. I picked him up and we went to a movie. When I dropped him off at his aunt's house afterwards, he wanted a kiss. I didn't want to give him one. He tried to convince me that I did. I can't remember his exact words, but his sharp-toothed smile is etched in my memory. The *sure you do* and the *just one kiss* and the *why else would you wear that denim mini skirt* grin. He tried to push his hand up my denim mini skirt, and I pushed his hand away. He used that hand to pull my keys out of the ignition and said he wouldn't give them back unless I gave him something. So, I opened my door and walked away from my car.

I walked towards a mid-century modern with double doors, intending to ring the doorbell. I hoped a woman would answer, and I'd tell her that this guy had taken my keys and wouldn't give them back. I don't know what I thought would happen after that, and honestly don't remember what *did* happen next. I only know I didn't have to ring the doorbell, and Toby didn't drive away with my car, or retreat to his aunt's house with my keys held hostage, or throw them down a sewer drain. All I know is he gave up and I was able to get back in my car and drive away alone. Unharmed.

I was lucky we were in a residential neighborhood, not some remote back road where there was nowhere to walk to, no doorbell to ring. I was lucky that I didn't like him enough to care what he thought, and we no longer went to camp together so I didn't care what he'd tell other people about me. I was also lucky that he hadn't really thought this through.

I never told anyone. It just seemed like something that happened to girls, and I didn't want to make a big deal out of it. It wasn't until #metoo—when I was fifty years old—that I realized Toby had tried to sexually assault me.

This is the part where I admit that my friend Dara actually gave me permission to tell the story of her being raped at a high school party when she was too drunk to resist or give consent. I just don't want to. I don't want to tell her story because I eventually learned it was another friend of mine who raped her. Who put his hand over Dara's mouth when she screamed.

There are many more people implicated in this story—witnesses, bystanders, friends—who did nothing. Many more people who I loved and trusted than my soul can bear. I think I might throw up now. I really will.

We were all looking back, Martin contended in our post-Ford testimony phone call. We were peeking into the fissures of memory, of time, of what we did and didn't do. Martin and I had this idea that any guy who date-raped a girl in high school at one of those parties, in one of those living rooms or garages or backyards or bedrooms, was looking into his own rearview mirror and realizing the damage he had wrought. He'd feel guilty and ashamed and might even seek out the woman and apologize. We also had this idea that anyone who knew about a guy assaulting a girl would realize the harm they'd done by protecting him, by not holding him accountable at the time, and they would do it now. They would come forward and say, "We know what you did, and it was terrible."

We had these ideas.

The Vail police asked the sixteen-year-old girl if she thought the boys might have viewed the oral sex as consensual. She had said numerous times that she was scared, that she felt pressured, that she was bullied, that the boys withheld her clothes until she gave them blow jobs, and yet the police wanted to know if she thought it was all one big misunderstanding.

"They were really drunk so they probably didn't know what's consensual and what's not and when to stop," the girl said.

Was Brett Kavanaugh too drunk to know what was consensual and when to stop? Was Carl, when he shoved his dick into an unconscious Sophia's mouth? Was my friend who raped Dara? Toby wasn't drunk when he tried to force sex on me by seizing my keys and barring my escape. What if I'd been too scared to leave my car and Toby had raped me? What would have been his excuse? And this is what I sometimes wonder: Does Toby ever think back on that event and realize it was I, not him, who prevented him from being a rapist?

At least that time.

When Dara told me about the boy, my friend, who raped her at a party in high school, I wrote back, "I'm so sorry this happened to you. I know intellectually that it was probably more common than I was aware of. I've been thinking about that a lot lately. All that was swept under the rug back then."

That's what really gnawed at the edges of my memory after Ford testified. Somehow, it was the first time I realized that boys and men I knew—friends—had probably committed sexual assaults. That other people I knew brushed it aside or covered for them. That there were monsters walking up and down our halls, past our lockers red and blue. They were in our classes, our cars, our homes, our living rooms. Maybe even our bedrooms.

Sophia didn't know that her best friend had told anyone about Carl assaulting her—not until I interviewed her. She wasn't surprised or mad. "When you think about the whisper network and its importance," Sophia said, "in those environments of privilege—whether it's a work environment where there's a definite power dynamic in place, or whether it's in Carl's house where he calls all the shots—there's no other way to protect yourself. There's no other way but to warn other people very directly."

There's no other way but for women to tell other women to stay away.

In the end, the Vail District Attorney didn't file criminal charges against any of the three boys in the hot tub, saying, "We couldn't prove the case beyond a reasonable doubt." One of the boys was expelled from Kent Denver for violating the school's code of conduct against mixing alcohol and sexual behavior. The media reported the other two boys also left the school, although it's not clear if they were expelled or voluntarily departed.

The father of the expelled boy vociferously defended his son, saying the girl was probably "embarrassed to be with multiple boys over the course of an evening," and fabricated the nonconsensual parts of the story. In other words, he was calling her a slut and a liar.

He also pointed out that the morning after the assault, the girl had texted a male friend that she had wanted to hook up with him the previous night, but knew he was drunk and didn't want to take advantage of him. The expelled boy's father said, "To me that doesn't sound like someone who has been traumatized."

There's no mention of this father being a trained trauma therapist, so I'm going to assume he's not. But I'd like to think you don't have to be a therapist to read his response and go, "Huh?" It implies that if she had been *truly* traumatized—as a victim of multiple assaults would be— she wouldn't have admitted to wanting consensual sex with a different guy. And she wouldn't have mentioned not wanting to take advantage of someone who was drunk. And what? She would have gone straight to the police about her own assault, instead, knowing it would lead to the whole messy ordeal playing out in the hallways at school, with people taking sides (as they eventually did), and her reputation getting dragged all over the place? Who the fuck *would* sign up for that? Christine Blasey

Ford did, out of a sense of civic duty, and received numerous credible death threats. Granted, the position of these three junior boys might not be as powerful as a Supreme Court judge, but in a small school where everyone knows everyone, there's nowhere to hide.

The girl wasn't even the one who told the school administration; it was her friend. He probably thought he was doing the right thing and wanted to see those guys punished. But the reality is, the girl's well-meaning friend stole her autonomy from her again. See, that's an often overlooked aspect of sexual assault: when the choice to give your body to another person has been ripped from you, you should at least have control over when to talk about it.

Martin now knows Carl raped Sophia because I told him. Looking back, he's pretty sure he was at that party at Carl's house. The realization left him appalled, sickened, nauseous, angry. He started replaying the night in his head. How it started with him feeling so very free and important and cool because he was invited to this exclusive event at Carl's house, and how it ended with Carl coming out of the bedroom, alone, without Sophia. The more he combed through his memory, the more cracks he found. He remembered something Carl had told him and Jeremiah after emerging from the bedroom: he said that he'd started to go down on Sophia but couldn't stand the smell, so he made her go shower.

"It was really important that he tell us he demeaned her," Martin realized in retrospect. But at the time, he was just a sixteen-year-old boy who wanted to fit in. He was another Gen X kid who had never heard the words date rape.

The angry father called his son's expulsion from Kent Denver a travesty and an example of gender bias gone wild. "The boys engaged in one sexual act and she engaged in three," he said, but *she* didn't get kicked out of school. "We have to move towards litigation."

He said suing Kent Denver was the only way to fix the unfairness his son had suffered. "The school has basically branded him, and I have to try to undo that."

A public database of court cases filed in Colorado doesn't reveal a single case involving Kent Denver and this issue. I don't know if the father's ire faded, or if he took the case to an attorney or judge who found it without merit, or if he decided to focus on righting the overturned ship of his son's life in more constructive ways.

Carl is now a generous philanthropist with a family. Harvey Weinstein supported AIDS research and numerous female political candidates. Russell Simmons was an ardent animal rights and gay rights activist. Toby has a wife and a wholesome-looking son at Yale. I've been trying to reckon with the idea that sometimes good men do bad things, and bad men do good things, but the more I think about it, the more the whole thing becomes a smoke screen. I can't quite work out if it matters if the man is, at his core, good or bad. What matters is what he did.

What do all these men tell themselves about what they did? Kavanaugh, Carl, the boys in the hot tub, Toby, the plethora of men named in #metoo and #timesup—are they having a reckoning, a real one? Because the public face of it doesn't reflect that. The stymied reflection is a tidal wave of denial, of "that never happened," or "it happened, but was consensual," or "I believe she was assaulted by someone, just not by me." Women seem to be the ones doing all the heavy lifting of reckoning.

And what of my friend, the one who committed an unthinkable act that causes me pain to think about, to write about, to picture? I hadn't seen or talked to him in over three years when Dara told me what happened. Was I supposed to call and tell him I know what he did thirty years ago, and it wasn't okay? I didn't think Dara had confided in me because she wanted me to act on her behalf. I believe she wanted to testify and for me to bear witness. But what if I was just another accomplice sweeping it under the rug?

"You do what is right for you," Dara said when I asked her. "I have no expectations for you to do one thing or another."

So, the story I tell myself is that I will see this man again someday. We will have dinner alone, and I will say, "There's something I need to talk to you about."

And I hope to god he'll say ... what, exactly? That he did it? Dara already told me he did it, so my heart has already been broken. Will he tell me "his side" of the story? Will he say he thought she was into it, or that he was so drunk himself he didn't know what he was doing, or that when she screamed, he thought she was screaming in passion, but they were at a party and were trying to be discreet? Or will he say, "I did that. I had no right, I have no good excuse, but I did it." Will I yell or cry or stare at him blankly and wish so badly I was someplace else, someplace where people I love didn't commit heinous acts against other people I love?

Will I forgive him?

Do I need to?

All these questions and mental gymnastics make me so fucking angry. I'm not just angry about what he did to Dara, but I'm angry that I'm thinking more about him than her. I'm angry that I have to re-evaluate everything I think I know and feel, that I have to reconcile the difference between the good and the bad, between the past and the present.

I often think of that once sixteen-year-old girl standing half-naked in a hotel hallway in Vail. I want to wrap her up in a down parka, a cashmere blanket, a flak jacket. She is now twenty-four, and I desperately wonder what happened in her life. Did she go to college and go to parties and manage to get good grades and have intimate relationships with other people, and not abuse drugs or booze or cut or starve herself or struggle with feelings of self-hatred? Does she question herself, still, like the Vail Police questioned her: Why didn't you leave? Could they have thought it was consensual? Or maybe she had her own reckoning. Maybe in 2017 the girl bravely—without shame, without fear—claimed the hashtag #metoo, and someone said, finally: I believe you.

Culture Shock

In 1983 I lost the part of Fastrada in our high school production of *Pippin* to Alicia Farber. Although, saying I "lost it" implies I was ever really "in the running," which is objectively doubtful. I was a talented dramatic actor, but not a great singer and only a so-so dancer. Alicia was a good actor, a decent singer, and a flawless dancer. She was also whip-smart, seemingly fearless, and beautiful—tall with just the right amount of booty and boobs, and a glamour-girl smile. I was cast in the chorus of Players, where my shortcomings were more easily overlooked. I couldn't even shimmy (and still can't). One time when I complained that I had no rhythm, Alicia said casually, "You should be Black."

I knew it was something only a Black person was allowed to say, and felt sort of "in" that she'd joke with me this way. Alicia was in the class ahead of me, one of five Black kids among the eighty-six graduates of Kent Denver Country Day's class of 1984. My class graduated 104 students, only one of whom was Black. Our sixteen-person *Pippin* cast featured two Black actors—both in lead roles—as well as a Latina lead. At the time, I didn't realize there was anything extraordinary about the play's level of inclusion. I also didn't understand that the reason I had so many friends of color was because we all existed on the social margins. I was a misfit because I'd spent the first half of my freshman year wearing preppy clothes and trying to like the "popular" kids, but found it was exhausting and didn't make me happy. Alicia was on the margins because she was "other," because she was Black, because she was on scholarship, and because she lived in the inner city. Even though we were othered together, we populated the periphery for very different reasons.

Alicia started Kent Denver as a sophomore, but that wasn't the beginning of her prep school odyssey. For her, it began in sixth grade at Graland Country Day, *the* elite school for grades K-9. There were other private elementary and middle schools in Denver, but most were parochial and relatively humble. Graland was also humble when it first began in 1924 as a preschool and kindergarten: its first classrooms were in a storefront at the Green Lantern Apartment building on East Colfax and 34th Street (sixteen years before the first appearance of the Green Lantern superhero, by the way). Throughout the 1920s, Graland added more grades and moved locations several times, until they landed at their current campus in Denver's Hilltop neighborhood.

These days, Hilltop is an upper-middle-class residential area. A mere three-and-a-half miles to downtown, it's considered Central Denver. But when Graland moved to Hilltop in 1928, it was mostly prairie grass and groundhogs. It was the country, a healthy *Sound of Music*-like learning environment, with all that sunshine and fresh air— the kind of place where rich people sent their kids.

Alicia grew up with her mother, Ella, five miles from Hilltop in Denver's historic Five Points neighborhood. Just north of downtown, the district was named for the intersection of where five streets met at the end of the streetcar line. In the late 1800s, a large concentration of Black rail workers settled along 22nd Street within Five Points. Mexican workers later settled on the west boundary along the Platte River, and Jewish and Japanese immigrants rounded out the population. But by the 1930's, Five Points was predominantly African American—and would stay that way for decades.

One of the reasons Five Points is a historically Black neighborhood is because discriminatory housing practices barred Black people from moving into other communities. Some of the racist mechanisms were super straightforward: housing covenants would specify "only persons of the Caucasians race shall own, use or occupy any dwelling or residence." Other methods were (slightly) sneakier. In 1933, the federal government graded neighborhoods based on how "loan worthy" they, and their residents, were. An "A" grade (shaded by the color green on a city map) meant the neighborhood was the Best (i.e., most likely to pay back a loan). B/blue was "still desirable," C/yellow = "Definitely declining," and D = "hazardous." The latter neighborhoods were shaded with red lines, hence the term "redlining." You might be shocked to hear that the redlined neighborhoods just *happened* to have primarily African American and Latino populations. Residents of redlined neighborhoods were denied home ownership loans, and were relegated to renting. The City of Denver added its own set of restrictive zoning laws to complete the Stay the Fuck Out trifecta: apartment buildings and boarding houses were banned in certain "desirable" neighborhoods. So, African Americans living in Five Points—whether they were renting or bought their own home before 1933—were stuck there.

But Five Points was no slum. It was home to thriving businesses like Rhythm Records and Sporting Goods, Rice's Tap Room and Oven, Melvina's Beauty Shop, Mallard's Grocery and Confectionary, and the Beaux Arts Rossonian Hotel. In the mid-twentieth century, Five Points boasted over fifty jazz clubs and dance halls that hosted jazz royalty like Count Basie, Billie Holiday, Duke Ellington, Louis Armstrong, and Miles Davis, earning its nickname "The Harlem of the West."

In 1959, Colorado was the first U.S. state to outlaw discriminatory housing practices with the Fair Housing Practices Act. Ironically, that curbing of segregation signaled the end of Five Points' glory years. Middle-class and affluent families moved out to other "desirable" neighborhoods. Between 1959 and1974, the Five Points population dropped from 32,000 to 8,700. Businesses closed. Housing fell into disrepair. In 1976, Alicia and Ella moved out of Five Points, too, but just two miles away, north of City Park. Their neighborhood was still regarded as the ghetto, the inner city, the "'hood."

Alicia attended public elementary schools, but Ella always wanted her to go to Graland Country Day. She was a single mom determined to give her daughter what she'd never had: an exceptional education and the opportunities it provided. Just in time to start sixth grade, Alicia got a full scholarship to Graland.

☩

It's important to fill in a blank here: why Alicia's mom was single, why Alicia had no dad. Her father, a white Jewish man, was attending the University of Denver in the mid-1960s when he met Ella. I'm not sure how they met, but do know that Temple Emanuel, Denver's oldest synagogue, was in Five Points. I know their margins overlapped. Ella discovered she was pregnant, and he bolted. Alicia told me his family said they'd disown him if he ever saw "that n----- woman and baby" again.

"We share that," Alicia said when I interviewed her in February 2020. She knew from my Facebook posts that I, too, was abandoned and rejected by my biological father.

Of course, my white father didn't reject me because of my race. He rejected me because I was inconvenient and unwanted—then, and now. My birthmother gave me away because it was shameful for an unmarried Catholic woman to have a baby. But maybe race does play a role in my story; maybe my biological parents knew that their white baby girl would quickly be snatched up because white baby girls were always in demand. In Alicia's case, however, it was clear from the very first moment of her life, her conception, that her race made her unwanted.

✣

Alicia grew up in primarily Black neighborhoods, and her family members were all Black, so Alicia considered herself Black—not biracial. "We weren't even called that back then," she said.

I've tried to remember what people of mixed-race heritage *were* called back then. The "best" (yikes) that I can come up with is mulatto, which is thought to derive from the Portuguese for "mule," which is pretty offensive. A bit of research turns up a lot of opinions about the correct ethnological term for people with both white and Black ancestry. Some people prefer the very nomenclature that others consider derogatory or limiting—including the terms biracial, mixed, and multiracial. It's not like there's a universal caucus making mutually agreed upon decisions for all people of mixed heritage, after all. As of this writing, "mixed race" seems to be the most widely accepted phrase, but I think it's wise to adopt whichever term the person I'm talking with and about uses to self-identify.

That's a very twenty-first century decision to make. In the late seventies and early eighties, Alicia didn't have access to a robust conversation about what to call herself, about who she is. "There wasn't a category for me," she said. "I was either considered a Black, or a Mexican, or white."

Right—the Mexican part: Alicia often passed for Mexican because of her lighter skin, fluency in Spanish, and straightened hair mandated by her grandmother. She told her granddaughter that the whiter you look, the better, and wouldn't allow Alicia to wear her hair natural. "The real racism of racism started in my own Black family," Alicia said.

As appalling as that sounds from the oh-so-enlightened twenty-first century, a lot of statistics—and lived experiences—shaped her grandmother's beliefs. Colorism, the belief that light-skinned Black people are superior to dark-skinned Black people, goes back to slavery. Lighter skinned slaves were more likely to work in the house, as opposed to the grueling fields. They were considered more intelligent, more skilled, and less savage. Keep in mind that their lighter skin wasn't due to some random gene expression: they were the products of white men raping their slaves. So, when lighter-skinned slaves were viewed as more intelligent, more skilled, and less savage, it's because slave owners were *literally* seeing themselves in them.

Colorism still persists in the twenty-first century. Numerous studies find that light-skinned Black people achieve higher rates of education, inhabit a higher socioeconomic rank and job status, and are less frequently incarcerated—or are incarcerated with less severe sentences—than their dark-skinned counterparts. As far as beauty standards go, light-skinned women are more likely to be beauty contestants and models, and be cast in advertisements, TV shows, and movies.

In other words: lighter skinned Black people have more advantages—and Alicia's grandmother wanted her to have *advantages*. Ella was always trying to turn that message around. Yes, she wanted Alicia to have advantages, too, but didn't believe Alicia had to be "less Black" to get them. That's obviously easier said than done in a systemically racist society—and especially when you're attending a mostly-white prep school.

Up until attending Graland, Alicia had never thought of herself as mixed, or poor, and never had any conscious issues about being abandoned by her white Jewish father. "But when I got to Graland, all that hit me," she said. "Because now I'm with all these rich white kids and all these Jewish kids."

It was the first time it really resonated that her father wanted nothing to do with her because of her race. On top of that, there were all these white kids who'd, somehow, never hung out with Black—or mixed—kids before, and didn't know what to make of her. When Ella picked Alicia up from school, the next day they asked, "Was that your nanny?" (My friend Martin, who also attended Graland, said, "You know, she might be putting a shine on even that. Kids thought she was Alicia's maid.")

"It was culture shock for me, and I guess I was culture shock for them," Alicia said. Two especially vivid moments of racism at Graland stick with Alicia and seem to fall into separate—but not unconnected—categories: the "Whoops/I'm such a dumbass I don't realize what's coming out of my mouth" kind, and the intentionally cruel "Yeah, I'm a racist, what of it?" kind. One happened when she was in sixth or seventh grade. Alicia and three other kids had gotten in trouble and had to stay after school to clean the blackboards and erasers. (This sounds hopelessly old fashioned now, like we might as well be in a one-room schoolhouse on the prairie.) The four were en route to do their duty—Alicia and one walking in front, and two boys in back—all complaining about their punishment.

"Yeah, that's n----- work!" said a boy behind Alicia.

She turned and gave him a stone-faced glare. He quickly said, "But we don't mean you."

It wasn't the first or last time Alicia would hear that caveat on the heels of a classmate throwing out the n-word: *We don't mean you.*

"But you mean my mama?" Alicia code-switched when telling me this part of the story. "You mean my whole family?" Her aunts and uncles and cousins and grandma and grandfather, who'd run the best-known barbershop in Five Points. "Whaddaya' mean, you don't mean me?"

Alicia's linguistic code switching is both the practical and metaphorical manifestation of the dichotomous life she—and other people of color—lead. There is one way of being, of speaking, of acting in their home life where they were raised and perhaps still live, and another way when navigating the white world. Most teenagers experience this to some extent: we are a different person at home than at school or summer camp or at our part-time jobs. But for white kids, that split—that need to change how we present—is not because the color of our skin has deemed us less than. It's not a matter of survival.

✛

Popularity became very important to Alicia. She wanted to be "the one" person of color to move out of the periphery and break into the popular crowd. It doesn't take Freud to draw the connection between how she'd been discarded and deemed undesirable by her white father, and why she was hell-bent on being accepted by the white kids. She wanted to get invited to all *the* parties. One of those parties occurred in eighth grade at a classmate's mansion (or his parents' mansion, at least) with a swimming pool, in Cherry Hills Village. Cherry Hills Village is just south of the Denver city limits, and not only the wealthiest neighborhood in Colorado, but one of the most affluent in the United States. It's the kind of neighborhood where Greek fountains embellish circular driveways and marble foyers boast grand staircases. The grounds (yes, they have *grounds)* are dotted with swimming pools and horse stables. If *Dynasty* had actually been filmed in Denver instead of Southern California, this is where it would have been set. To say that Cherry Hills was worlds away from Alicia's house north of City Park is a ridiculous understatement.

Alicia's mother was working the day of the pool party, so her friend Bettina's mom planned to come *waaaay* over to pick up Alicia. Alicia sat in her house ready with her swimsuit, but no one ever came. There was no texting, no cellphones, no way to reach people in these circumstances. You just had to sit and *wait.* Eventually, Bettina called from the party. Alicia could tell from Bettina's voice that she felt really bad and was dancing around whatever the truth was.

Finally, Bettina said, "I'm really sorry, Alicia, but they said you can't come because you're Black."

A boy standing near Bettina grabbed the phone away from her and said, "That's right, no n------ allowed!" and hung up.

Alicia was destroyed. She called her mother at work, crying hysterically. "I think my mother thought I was suicidal." Ella warned Alicia, "Don't you go doing anything stupid," and instructed her to go to her grandmother's house right away. But Alicia didn't go. She was too devastated.

These days, we like to throw around the term "teachable moment," and this became one. Literally. Ella told the Graland administration what had happened, making it abundantly clear this was not okay. On Monday, the history teacher (who Alicia said bore a remarkable resemblance to Charles Bronson) said, "Now let's talk about this party that happened over the weekend."

I assumed this was absolutely humiliating for Alicia, to have one of her most painful adolescent moments amplified as a classroom lesson. But she said the teacher made it perfectly clear *who* should be embarrassed. Charles Bronson directly called out the kid who threw the party, and told him he should be ashamed. From that time on—and all the way through high school at Kent Denver Country Day—that kid personally invited Alicia to any party at his parents' mansion in Cherry Hills.

✛

The Kent Denver campus is also in Cherry Hills, on two hundred acres of former farmland, with two lakes and pristine views of the Rocky Mountains. When Alicia started Kent for her sophomore year, it required at least a forty-minute city bus ride just to get to the corner of Colorado Boulevard and Hampden Avenue, the entrance to Cherry Hills. The city bus didn't go beyond that. Sometimes Alicia walked the remaining one-and-a-half miles to school, and sometimes she caught a ride from a friend. One day, after school let out, she was going the opposite way, with a friend giving her a ride to the bus stop. Several girls were in the car, the way teenagers used to pile in like clowns in a Volkswagen. Alicia was sitting between the driver, Ann, and another girl in front. A car cut them off and Ann slammed on the brakes. A girl named Diana in the backseat, yelled, "Hit the n-----!"

There was a full stop silence in the car.

Alicia looked at Ann and said, "Let me out."

"No, Alicia." Ann was kind, not from a prejudiced family, and Alicia knew from her soft voice that she felt terrible. "We're not at your bus stop yet."

Alicia also knew if she didn't get out of that car, she "was going to get in the back seat and fuck that girl up." But Ella had always told her: You are the Black girl, and they expect you to be like that, so you can't be like that. You are the one person who cannot be like that. So, Alicia repeated, "Let me out of this car."

The girl sitting next to her scooted out, and Alicia walked the rest of the way to the bus stop. I wonder if it ever occurred to any of the girls that the one who should get out and walk was Diana.

✟

In June of 2020, I received an email from the Kent Denver Head of School addressed to all parents and alumni. He wrote:

> In the last few weeks, we have been reminded, again, of the impact of systemic racism on our fellow citizens, and we have witnessed the deaths of Ahmaud Arbery, Breonna Taylor and George Floyd. As a school founded on the core values of Integrity, Respect, Personal Growth, Community, and Wisdom, we cannot observe what is happening and remain silent. Silence is not what we teach our students about equity, responsibility, and leadership. Silence is not what has defined us for almost 100 years.

He offered, "Parents who would like to participate in conversations around race, equity, and inclusion are invited to join the Navigating Circles Affinity Group that meets quarterly during the school year."

The group had formed nearly four years earlier, right after the 2016 Presidential election. "Implicit Bias" was discussed in the first meeting. Other topics over the years included: "Raising Anti-Racist Kids," "Intent vs. Impact," "Talking About Race," "Having Difficult Conversations," and "The Challenges of Parenting Children to Be Empathetic Adults." I can assure you *none* of this was being discussed when I was a student at Kent. Like, I don't remember a single conversation about race. So, when I read, "Silence is not what has defined us for almost 100 years," I think: Well, it kind of *has*. Because silence about racism has defined white spaces for well over one hundred years.

Zero multicultural programming existed when I was at Kent. We studied white, Eurocentric history. The authors on our English reading lists were mostly (entirely?) white men. There wasn't a single African-American teacher in the *entire* school. In the 1980s, there was no push against our ivy-covered walls to include the stories and voices of people of color. While Kent Denver recruited a few Black and Latino and Native America students, the curriculum and culture still reflected back that anything worth learning—and anyone worth teaching it— was white.

✛

The story I wanted to tell about Alicia was what it was like being a Black girl in a mostly-white prep school. It turned out that was only one part of the bumpy landscape of her adolescence. Alicia's story of being "the Black girl" took a radical turn the summer before her sophomore year at Kent, when Ella was diagnosed with breast cancer.

Alicia became consumed with taking care of her mother. Her Aunt Glory helped pay the bills, but it was up to Alicia to cook, clean, shop, and do laundry. She also had to feed her mother, as well as help administer her chemotherapy. A friend of Ella's, who was a nurse, showed Alicia how to care for the catheter. "Why was she teaching me?" Alicia said. "I was fifteen fucking years old, a child."

Years later, when Alicia confronted her aunts and uncles and older cousins, they told her that she was so smart and competent, they assumed she didn't need help. "I had a double life," Alicia said. "I was a good girl as far as my mother and family knew—taking care of my mother when she was at home. But I was a bad girl, otherwise—sex and drugs and rock and roll."

Ella was in and out of the hospital, and Alicia stayed with Aunt Glory or at friends' houses when Ella wasn't home. Her friend Darcy lived close to Kent in a mid-century modern ranch where I attended many a laid-back stoner party. Darcy's father had died during her junior year, so it's easy to see how her mom, Zita, wanted to give this girl with no father and a dying mother a soft place to land.

In August of 1983, before Alicia's senior year, Ella went back into the hospital, where she remained until she died in November. But before Ella left this earth, she arranged for Alicia to permanently live with Darcy and Zita. Alicia doesn't know the details, but Zita was a judge and certainly understood the legalities required. She knew it had to be official, and not just an act of love.

During those last months in the hospital, Ella would always grab Alicia's hand before she left and say, "God, please just let me see my pretty baby graduate." But Ella never made it to any of Alicia's graduations, not from high school at Kent Denver, not from college at Northwestern, and not from graduate school at Loyola, where Alicia earned a master's in Social Work—all the educational opportunities Ella had wanted for her smart, beautiful, talented daughter.

✢

Here's what I, quite unfortunately, remember about the day Alicia's mom died: It was a Friday and we had a performance of *Pippin* that night. Throughout the day, I had wondered if Alicia would still perform. How could she, I wondered, be the evil, sexy, back-stabbing Fastrada, shimmying around and insincerely asking everyone to "Spread a Little Sunshine," when her mother, her life, her light, had just gone out? When Alicia had just become an orphan? I didn't know about that kind of grief back then—not like I do now—and that sometimes you just push through it. You do what needs to be done if, for no other reason, than because your mama would want you to stand on that stage and give the best damn performance of your life.

At some point, for one terrible moment on the day Alicia's mom died, I stopped thinking about all that. I don't know exactly what I was thinking—other than nothing? That evening I walked into the room where the cast was putting on makeup and ensuring our costumes fit just right, and no one was laughing. There was no boom-box music, no flirting, none of the usual pre-show energy. I jokingly exclaimed to the whole room, "Wow, who died?"

It took me two seconds to realize what I had done, to re-remember why we were all so somber, to look over at Alicia and say, "Oh my god, I'm so sorry!" and a bunch of other blather to try to explain away the unexplainable.

A few years later, when I was home from college for the summer—about five years before my own mom died—I went into a Taco Bell and found Alicia behind the counter. It was a huge disconnect to see her there. Not because she was working fast food—I'd worked in a burger joint, myself—but because she was so damn pretty in that stupid brown uniform, so much more sparkly than anyone and anything around her. I don't remember what I ordered, just that when I went to pay for it, Alicia pushed my food towards me and whispered, "It's all right."

She may not have remembered the night of my blunder, or maybe she did, but I took solace in that moment, in Alicia telling me things were all right.

✛

At Northwestern, Alicia had biracial friends for the first time in her life. "They thought I was a little crazy, like a stalker," she said, because as soon as she found out someone was biracial, she immediately wanted to know everything about them. She immersed herself in learning what it means to be mixed, and even did a research project on it, interviewing other biracial students (and thus giving her a legitimate reason to stalk them). Prior to college, though, Alicia felt like an alien. "I felt like there was no one like me."

She also happened to attend college in the same city where her biological father lived. She attempted to contact him, but never heard back. However, Zita (in Denver) received a letter from an attorney instructing Alicia to leave her biological father and his family alone or they'd get a restraining order. I received a similar letter from my biological father's attorney, with slightly more ominous language: *He'll do whatever is necessary to protect his family,* (prompting a friend to ask, "Is he going to have you wacked?"). A quick consult with my attorney confirmed it wasn't an official cease and desist, and they couldn't really get a restraining order, because I hadn't done anything illegal, threatening, or harassing. I'm sure Judge Zita realized this, too. Alicia's response was, "Really? So that's what we're doing now?" which is shorthand for "What a cowardly motherfucker," which also means, *I've been rejected again.*

✛

Alicia is now the adoptive mother to a little girl. Her daughter's birthmother has six children who have been adopted by four different families. Three of the four families, including Alicia, are committed to the siblings knowing each other. They're spread out in all corners of the Chicago area, but manage to coordinate gatherings at least four times a year.

Alicia is also a transracial adoption specialist, providing support and training to white families adopting children of color. Even the most woke, well-meaning white people can be uninformed about how to approach their child's race. Since its inception, transracial adoption has been plagued by White Savior Complex (I'm going to save this Black baby because I'm a good white person and I'm going to blog about it so everyone knowns how generous I am), and color blindness—pretending the child's race doesn't matter, or ignoring their Black heritage out of a desire to erase the pain of being abandoned by their biological parents.

Alicia believes she's been able to achieve so much because of attending Graland and Kent. Combined with living in a Black and Mexican neighborhood and being biracial, the experiences gave her the ability to move with confidence through a variety of social and professional circles, to travel to different countries, to walk into any room and not be made to feel like she doesn't belong. If she moved back to Denver, she'd even consider enrolling her daughter in one of those schools. "I've lived that life," she said. "I know how to navigate that, whereas my mother did not."

But from where I'm standing, it looks like Ella did a pretty good job.

I interviewed Alicia before COVID-19 shut down the world, before Breonna Taylor and Dreasjon Reed and George Floyd were murdered by police officers, before the protests and riots and outrage that ensued, and before Kent Denver sent out an email saying, "Silence is not what has defined us for almost 100 years." I was aware of how often Black people are asked to serve as educators for their white friends, and profusely thanked Alicia for taking the time and energy to talk to me.

"I'm very open about this because ... me telling a story like this, there's somebody who needs to hear it," she said. "There always is, and there always will be. I see that as my civic duty."

I now want to ask her if she still feels so *positively* about her experiences at white prep school. If it was still all worth it. If any other feelings have surfaced since Ms. Taylor and Mr. Reed and Mr. Floyd were killed. But I don't. I don't, because I figure she's got her plate full. She's got her own fear and rage and single parenthood and unemployment. I suspect she doesn't need me, a white person, asking her to explain how things are.

A Letter to Frederic Lyman and the Plethora of Other Private School Teachers Who Sexually Abused Their Students

Dear Mr. Lyman,

You might already be thinking how weird it is that we're referring to you as "Mr. Lyman," instead of as "Rick." However, "Mr. Lyman" is the proper way for high school students to refer to their teacher. At small, private schools—boarding and day—students sometimes end up calling teachers by their first names, under certain circumstances. But we now see that the moment you started using your first name with us, signing our graded papers *Love, Rick*, we were already on a dangerous descent towards inappropriate familiarity. We haven't been your students for nearly forty years, but this is one small impropriety we can go back and correct.

You were our literature teacher. You wooed us, you preyed on us, you groomed us, you harassed and abused us. You did it at Phillips Andover Summer Academy in 1979 and 1980; you did it at Beaver Country Day from 1979 to 1980; you did it at Choate Rosemary Hall from 1980 to 1982; you did it at Kent Denver Country Day from 1982 to 1984. Most of us were sixteen when you started in on us. One of us was fourteen.

We can now recognize your *modus operandi*, especially at the boarding schools: You'd invite us over to your apartment outside of class. You'd serve us wine and rum-spiked tea. You'd help us break curfew and sneak off campus. You'd take us to the library off campus, to concerts, to dinner. You held our hands and walked with your arm around us.

You were so good looking, with your blond hair and blue eyes, your slightly athletic build, your preppy style. Early on, when you were grooming us at Phillips Summer Academy, you were what some might call "a perfect gentleman." Even amid the poetry and wine and breaking curfew to go off campus, you didn't try to coerce us into sleeping with you. Not then. We thought we were in love. But we also sensed there was something deeply weird about our relationship, and it frightened us. The benefit of time and maturity helps us see and hold compassion for the battle that was waged in our heads and our hearts and our bodies—between hormones and gut instinct, our need to be loved, and our sense of wrong.

We left Phillips Summer Academy and returned home to start our junior year of high school. You wrote to us there, at our parents' home. You said you'd love to kidnap us for a weekend or part of our winter break, to wine and dine us, to treat us like a queen. How bold of you to write a letter like this to our parents' home! We know you were *probably* just being playful when saying you wanted to "kidnap" us. You weren't actually threatening physical abduction. But surely you realized it was illegal to give alcohol to minors, to tempt us to go out of town with you (even cross state lines), which inevitably would include sleepovers.

And surely you must have realized that your letter constituted blackmail. You said if we didn't take you up on your offer: "I'll be so frustrated I may never forgive you. I'll write terrible recommendations for you." You threatened to send us hate mail, to call us at obscure hours and "swear a bloody streak" (you actually specified the time you'd call, "i.e. 3am"). No, you did not physically abduct us, Mr. Lyman, but you held us emotionally hostage.

We wrote you back, but kept it cursory. Not overly friendly, but not overly distant either. We have all learned how to do this throughout our lives: micro-manage our behaviors to keep predators like you at bay. We know you did not appreciate this reply. You wanted us to be flattered and excited (as we were over the summer, when you were feeding us wine and poetry), so you admonished us in your next letter. You said our obligatory-style response with "far more facts than feeling" dampened the spirit of what was previously shared between us. "Oh well," you wrote, "so much for feeling the pangs of distance and time."

When you wrote this letter, you were teaching at Beaver Country Day in Newton, Massachusetts. There, you gave more of us alcohol, you smoked pot with us, you kissed and touched us in inappropriate ways. You pressured us to have sex with you. We told the administration at Beaver Country Day, the educators responsible for protecting us. They didn't fire you; they didn't call the cops. They let you resign. They even gave you a letter of recommendation. "Passing the trash," we'd later learn this practice was called.

This is a crime aided by many accomplices. Silence, apathy, and inaction were their crimes.

You spent the next summer again teaching at Phillips Summer Academy, where you again gave us alcohol and held our hands and walked with your arm around us. You sang to us and tried to put your lips to ours, your tongue inside our mouths. We didn't want your lips on our lips, your tongue in our mouths. The only way you could get close to us was when we were sleeping. One night on a camping trip when you were our chaperone, we awoke to find you stroking and kissing our arms. It was all we could do to pretend to be asleep, to hope you would just go away.

We didn't all attend Phillips Summer Academy that year. After the letter you sent to our parents' house declaring you wanted to kidnap us, we instead attended Harvard summer session for high schoolers. You wrote us at Cambridge, starting with *I miss you so much.* You urged us to come out for a night on the town, or for an "adventure" to Ashby. Ashby is a small Massachusetts town on the New Hampshire border, forty-two miles west of Andover, and fifty miles northwest of Harvard. It is not in-between or even close to the two towns. It is distinctly out of the way. Ashby has about 3,000 residents, one public library (you did like taking us to libraries!), no museums, and limited restaurants. We can only guess what your intended "adventure" included.

We did what women have always done with men like you: We tried to keep from making you angry and following through on your threats to stalk us and swear a bloody streak. We said we'd meet up with you, hoping to get you off our back. Later, we reneged, saying our parents were in town. And alas, Mr. Lyman, you did exactly what you threatened: you called us at all hours of the day and night, harassing us. Eventually, we put a note on the phone in our Harvard dorm that said: "If Rick calls, we died."

The last letter you wrote us at Harvard summer session— before our senior year of high school—was dated July 17, 1980. (We kept these letters; did you not think we would?) You typed out your disappointment on lined yellow paper. "I can't believe your attitude," you started. "What did I do to deserve silence and the cold shoulder?"

We will tell you what you did, Mr. Lyman, since you seem to be ... "baffled," was the word you used. You threatened us and stalked us and punished us for not engaging in a relationship with you. We'd also like to point out what a fucking weird question this is for a twenty-eight-year-old man to ask of a teenage girl he'd known for a year. We didn't know this then, but we do now: Teenagers—students—don't owe their teachers anything other than studying. Showing up for class. Taking tests. Speaking respectfully. We are not responsible for your loneliness, fear, desires, and other intimate pathos.

In that last letter, you told us: "If you think I wanted any sort of love relationship you're way off target." You actually claimed that you never desired anything other than friendship and that our rejection of said friendship left you "truly pierced."

Mr. Lyman, you certainly wouldn't be the last man to try to gaslight us in the face of our rejection.

I was just kidding.

You're overreacting.

I'm happily married.

You're so sensitive.

You're crazy.

It's always confusing when men do this, regardless of our age or their age. We want you to know that because you were an adult in a position of authority, it really messed with our reality. It left us deeply unsettled for years.

Because Beaver Country Day didn't fire you and they gave you a letter of recommendation after learning of your improprieties, you went on to teach at Choate Rosemary Hall for two years. Choate is a boarding school, so we didn't have our parents to look out for us. We only had our teachers and each other. That was your responsibility, Mr. Lyman, to protect us, and you did precisely the opposite.

During your first year at Choate, you slipped creepy notes under our doors. You were touchy-feely and clingy with us. One night we woke to find you in our dorm room spinning in circles (no, after all these decades, we still don't understand why). We were so freaked out that we begged to switch out of your class, although we didn't tell the administration our true reason for doing so.

You invited us to your apartment for music, poetry, dinners, drinks. And sex. Sex in your apartment, sex in your car, sex in your parents' house during a ski vacation. Sex with more than one of us—you had (at least) two of us in rotation. We heard rumors about each other but didn't know for sure. Our relationships were supposed to be secret—that was part of the thrill, the romance of it all.

You might have been able to continue your seductions/violations/crimes indefinitely at Choate, except in March of 1982, we ended up in the emergency room of Yale New Haven Hospital with a herpes infection contracted from you. Our parents became aware of our so-called "relationship" with you. They insisted that you be fired. But what did Choate— our school that we trusted, that our parents trusted—do? They didn't report you to the police. They let you finish out the school year. They let you resign, and they gave you a letter of recommendation for your next job at Kent Denver Country Day in Colorado.

Here we have another accomplice, Charles Twichell, the dean of faculty at Choate. He wrote a positive recommendation for you with this veiled caveat: "Rick likes to meet his students on even terms, to mix with them as colleagues." He said that you had an "easy familiarity" with students and a "reluctance" to accept appropriate conventions in the student-teacher relationship. Mr. Twichell hoped that one day you would "learn the professional advantages of keeping a little more distance in the ranks." It's all so oblique—especially in a letter, over the phone, where the headmaster at Kent Denver Country Day couldn't see Mr. Twichell raise an eyebrow or tilt his head in a way that would convey, "I'm not saying it, but you know what I'm saying, right?"

There's also the possibility that Mr. Twichell didn't care. This kind of abuse had been part of the culture of Choate and other private schools for decades. That's the other reason you thought this was all acceptable. There were so many men before you, alongside you, after you, at so many private schools who'd done the same: Brian Davidson, David Cobb, Richard Keller, Stephen Wicks, Alexander Theroux, H. Schuyler Royce, John Joseph, Bill Maillet, Kenneth Mills, Chip Lowery, Adam Hardej, Jean-Marc Dautrey, Angus Mairs, Bjorn Runquist, Bill Cobbett, Jaime Rivera-Murillo, Chuck Timlin, Rick Schubart, Peter Hindle, Bryce Lambert, Dick Shoemaker, Bob Ashe, Mark Petersen, Samuel Crawley, Deonte Huff … we could go on, but we can't go on, because there are over a hundred. Over one hundred that we know of, over a hundred sexual predators at private schools who've been exposed in the last ten years.

We, the writers of this letter, were girls when our trust was shattered, but we hold hands with—we hold hearts with—our brothers, the boys, who were abused by men like you. Yes, *like you*. The sex, the gender, the genitalia is irrelevant. The piercing of our souls is what matters. The breaking of our lives.

In your resignation letter, you said that you were leaving "for the sake of Choate Rosemary Hall and for me." You did not say you were leaving for our sake, us girls on the verge of womanhood who would be forever affected by your manipulations. You said during your remaining time at Choate "I promise not to be the source of any new rumors or incidents." As if that's all that had occurred, that you'd been snagged in some ugly rumor mill. You didn't get it, and why would you? No one forced you to face the severity of your actions.

We wonder why you decided to move halfway across the country to Colorado. Did you hope that a change of scenery would put you back on the straight and narrow? Kent Denver Country Day isn't a boarding school, so parents are involved in students' lives. You applied for a job teaching middle school. We were twelve and thirteen and fourteen years old, so maybe you thought you'd be less tempted by such young girls living at home? Or, maybe, you moved away from the scenes of your crimes and towards younger girls—less worldly girls—because you thought it would be easier to manipulate us.

We were in eighth grade, and you were our thirty-year-old English teacher when you started writing personal notes on our graded papers, signed with your first name. Your notes eventually became flirtatious. At the end of the year, you wrote in our yearbook: "A pretty exposed place to write ... all that I'd like ... but I think you know how very special you are to me."

To someone reading this for the first time, your brazenness is probably mind boggling. Flirting on our papers, in our yearbook! But we know what you were doing. You were testing the waters with us, and you were testing the waters of the entire environment. What could you get away with?

We didn't respond to your yearbook note—or any of your notes on our papers—and didn't tell anyone in a position of authority. Our parents never saw those graded English papers, they never read our yearbook and said, "What the holy hell is this?" We commenced from eighth grade to ninth grade, to a different part of campus than where you taught. We had almost no contact with you for the first part of freshman year, just seeing you across the dining hall from time to time.

We have obsessively wondered where you got the idea that any of this was okay. You were a literature teacher, so we assume you've read *Lolita*. We also assume you believed, like many others, that Dolores seduced Humbert Humbert and he was helpless to her wiles. (We refer to her by her given name, Dolores, not the name Humbert Humbert thrust upon her.) We must say, Mr. Lyman, we're terribly disappointed that you took away such an unsophisticated reading of the text. We all know Humbert is the classic unreliable narrator (he tells us that he's a murderer and a liar!). Nabokov did such a masterful job in creating this unreliable narrator that many readers believed Humbert when he said Dolores, a twelve-year-old, seduced him. But Nabokov also provided cracks through which the astute reader could see Humbert was full of shit. We knew he was a rapist because he had to drug Dolores in order to have sex with her. The next day, pain was evident on her face, in her walk. Dolores called him a brute and threatened to tell the police he'd raped her. Humbert tried to convince himself, to convince us, she was joking. He exploited her mother's death by telling Dolores she had nowhere to go, no one to go to, ensuring her captivity in his prison.

Mr. Lyman, is this the man you wanted to model yourself after?

In the last few years, more secrets about your tenure at Kent Denver Country Day have been revealed. Even though you were a middle school teacher, you coached upper school boys' hockey, where we—sixteen- and seventeen-year-old girls—were the team managers and fans, and you took full advantage of our proximity. You proposed dates, alcohol, sex. We talked to our friends about you over coffee late at night, contemplating losing our virginity to you.

We also now know that while you were teaching in Colorado, you were still carrying on with the two of us from Choate, the ones you'd had in rotation the previous year. You wrote us love letters and called us frequently; you sent us plane tickets to visit you in Denver during our breaks. We once tried to break up with you, and you threatened to kill yourself.

Our flying to Colorado to sexually gratify you wasn't enough. Seven months after signing our eighth-grade yearbook at Kent Denver Country Day, you sent us a Christmas card. You knew it was risky, you wrote, but urged us to "take a chance" by getting together with you off campus. You wanted to take us skiing, or meet you for dinner and wine. Considering we were fourteen, it's unlikely we'd be served wine in a restaurant, suggesting that you were inviting us to your apartment.

You were pushing the boundary further than ever before. We wonder, were you just *that stupid*, that it never occurred to you that our parents might discover your card? You must have known it was inappropriate; you'd been warned of and let go from your two previous jobs because of your predatory behavior. But you didn't suffer severe consequences. You were never charged with engaging in sex with minors under your supervision, and you weren't fired, and you were given letters of recommendation. Perhaps you believed this sort of conduct was merely *frowned upon*, but not absolutely forbidden. That was the message you were given by people in authority, by your accomplices.

Your Christmas card and its suggestions freaked us out. We didn't know how to handle it. We can still viscerally feel this liminal place of a girl in her first year of high school. We don't want to think of ourselves as children. We share everyday space with seniors who drive and drink and have sex, and want to be seen as their peers. We don't want to run to our parents, but we also don't have the skills to deal with a sexual predator on our own.

We left your card lying around our house. Our dad found it. He went to the Kent Denver administration and demanded you be fired. Kent Denver did not immediately fire you. They insisted that you get counseling (oh, to be a fly on that therapist's wall!), and cease interacting with us outside of school hours. They said they wouldn't renew your contract or give you any sort of recommendation and suggested you not pursue any more jobs in teaching. But they did let you finish out the school year. This allowed you to glare at us from across the dining room for five months. It made us feel terrible, like we had betrayed you.

You moved back to Boston. You weren't finished with us girls from Choate. You stalked us at college. You left notes at our dorm. You spoke to our friends. You threatened us. You hit us. The bruise from the black eye still lies deep in our memory. We went to our father's house for protection, but you tracked us down there. You came to the door. We truly can't believe your chutzpah/stupidity/it'll take a team of psychoanalysts to understand why you did this. Our father threatened to call the cops. You promised you'd leave us alone *if* we returned everything you'd ever given us: the letters, the jewelry, the photos. The evidence. When we complied with your final demand, Mr. Lyman, you finally left us alone.

We've lived with all this for two, three, four decades. Some of us told our friends, our partners, our therapists. Some of us told no one. We locked away how you took advantage of our trust, our youth, our inexperience, our need to feel exceptional. But buried secrets have a way of pushing to the surface. We started talking about you and your ilk. We talked about it on social media and to lawyers and to the press. Our schools from long ago, the ones charged with educating and nurturing and protecting us, finally called for our voices. They launched investigations to find out how many voices there were.

Not all our voices came forward. Some of us didn't want to speak of what happened. We wanted to keep it buried away. Not all of us heard the call. We also know, in our most tender places, that not all of us are still here, walking this earth, with our voices to be heard. But enough voices spoke that people listened. And while late is better than never, it was too late for you to be held accountable.

Because, Mr. Lyman, by the time all your crimes became very, very public, the statutes of limitations had long expired. You would not be tried for luring minors under your supervision into sex, for coercion, and assault and battery. You would not even admit to the enormity of what you had done. When contacted by the *New York Times* with and about the letters you'd written to us when we were sixteen (remember the one saying you wanted to kidnap us? Remember the one telling us how we were crazy to think you wanted more than friendship?), you said, "In re-reading these letters nearly 40 years after writing them, I see the ramblings of a lovesick young man who was 27 years old at the time. However, my lapse in judgment was inexcusable. I breached the trust and overstepped the boundaries between student and teacher.

Due to my own immaturity, I considered my students to be peers and friends, which was a mistake that I will regret for the rest of my life. I am deeply sorry for any pain or discomfort my actions may have caused."

Mr. Lyman, we don't know who you think you're fooling. Are you even fooling yourself? *Lovesick*, as if you were powerless to your own emotions and desires. Was your so-called immaturity also the reason you pursued us when we were only fourteen? Why you stroked our arms while we slept, why we woke to find you spinning in our dorm room, why you fucked us? Was it why you gave us herpes and a black eye? We are well aware, Mr. Lyman, that you didn't comment on any of that. You only commented on the letters, the *evidence* you didn't have the foresight to retrieve early in your crimes.

You did not suffer, and you did not pay for what you did to us. Oh sure, after all this became public in 2017 your social media profiles disappeared for a short period of time. But they are now back up. As far as we can tell from your LinkedIn profile, Kent Denver was your last teaching job. You are now the president of an executive coaching firm, and you volunteer as a kids' soccer coach. On Facebook, your "likes" are: anything outdoors, skiing, coaching, and kids. We can't imagine how or why you, a person accused of sexual misconduct against minors, would include "kids" as one of your likes, but there it is. There *you* are. Like most sexual predators, you've gone on to live a relatively unaffected life.

But we are not unaffected—not any of us who you and your ilk abused. We have borne intense shame. We have starved ourselves. We have pumped our blood full of alcohol and drugs. We spent decades unable to trust others, unable to be intimate. We have been tormented by nightmares. We have been harrowed by the constant fear of being attacked, or dying, at any time. We have struggled with feeling that life is a meaningless void, and perhaps it would be better to die. We have doubted ourselves—what we did and didn't do, what we did and didn't have done to us. We have thought it was our fault, that we were violated because we were bad people.

We were not bad people. Moralists and ethicists debate if a person is more or less than the sum of their actions, if their crimes can be fully atoned for, if there is ever enough good to make up for the bad a person has done. We don't claim to hold the definitive answers to these questions. We know this, Frederic Lyman: what you did to us was wrong. You caused fissures deep in the core of our souls. And your apology forty years later—only when confronted with the press and pressure to issue one, not of your own volition—does not reconcile with the enormity of your wrongs, of the guilt and fear and turmoil and dread you instilled in us. And it most certainly does not indicate you'd sought real help to understand your motivations. This is what chills us the most. That by foregoing this examination and insight into your crimes, you were, and are, likely to commit them again.

And if you, and those like you, do, our voices will shout out. We are getting stronger by the minute.

Sincerely,

All the Women Who Were Once Girls

Part II

Let us not then speak ill of our generation …
Let us not speak well of it, either.
Let us not speak of it at all.

—Samuel Beckett

Long and Thin

Bobby was fifteen and long and thin in a body that had shot up around him too fast. Long fingers wrapped around the lacrosse stick's metal shaft, his brown eyes with lashes long like a girl's watching the ball rocket downfield, curly bangs grazing cheeks like a cherub masking how promiscuous everyone said he was, sleeping with the loosest girl in school and drinking beer and smoking pot with no responsibilities, no cares.

I had no use for his kind.

Bobby was eighteen and long and lean, with a sinewy body that he moved like a ballet dancer aware of the space above and below him, but casual, like a jungle cat stretched out on the bed next to me, chestnut curls pushed past cloudy eyes, lips ripe like an heirloom tomato musing over the beauty of the human body—my human body—a work of art, his words were true and the others' were false, his body was hard and introduced my mouth to new tastes, salty, of the earth.

We never fell in love.

Bob was twenty-two, denim-dressed knees pointing to the night sky, ass on damp grass, Pomp and Circumstance behind us now. The moon shining past his eyes—light so bright it washed out his skin, erased his features so he was dream-like, ghost-like—his voice deep and throaty he wondered if he would ever find it, real love, was he too old or too young to know true happiness, to know who he would become.

We went our separate ways.

Robert was thirty-four in black and white, a sparse beard creeping across cheekbones now angled and defined. He towered above his wife, hair straight and long the color of saffron, a daughter in his arms with lanky limbs, the cheeks of a cherub and saffron hair, and printed beneath this photo was the date of his birth and the date of the day the thin, metal pipe shot off the back of a truck in front of him, penetrating his dusty windshield like a bullet through his throat, oh how he wrapped his long fingers around the cold steel and with one last jerk pulled the pipe out of his neck.

He left a gaping hole.

Bobby was seventeen, long and languid against the wall, my cheek pressed against his chest pulsing against my skin, his eyes—my eyes— his mind—my mind cloudy with drink, relaxed with weed, thin fingers grazing the nape of my neck, lips near my ear speaking in a voice deep and throaty that we leave this room, these people, this party, find someplace private.

We were alone.

A Change in Altitude

It's spring break 1986 and I'm staying at my dad's house in Denver instead of my mom's house in Denver because my mom hates Leon, my boyfriend for the last two years. My mom hates Leon because he's older and because I took the first semester off from college to live with him and because he deals coke. So, I'm staying at my dad's house instead of my mom's house or even at Leon's house, because Leon has a new house and a new roommate and even though we're technically still together, being in different states for the last few months makes it impossible to be close now. We're like a thread split in half, unable to tightly re-twine.

The first night at my dad's house I take off all my clothes and sit in the steam room. For the last three months I've been jumping out of my skin to escape college in Portland, but when I think about what I've come back to—who's out there waiting for me or maybe never even noticed I was gone—it's a jumbled mess of faces and names moving from club to club, from party to party, and makes me just want to be alone in the moist heat. My dad says that the steam room is a good place for him to work things through, so I watch the fog circle around the light and try hard to think about all my problems—guys and sex and getting my first ever "D" and all that rain and the coke dealing disaster and the bloody noses I got *after* I quit—but I can't get close to any of it. It seems like the distance would be good, but it just makes me feel ripped apart from everyone and everything.

I didn't mean to sell coke at school, but when my R.A. found out Leon dealt back home, she said I should start selling in our dorm. Selling makes you feel like you have control over other people even if you don't have control over yourself, so I started moving a quarter here or there, never more than an eight-ball. When the Dean of Students heard a rumor that someone on my floor was dealing, my R.A. refused to rat me out and was fired and kicked off campus. I don't know if that was out of loyalty to me or because she thought I'd rat her out, too.

After I get out of the steam room, I call Leon. We just saw each other—he picked me up from the airport and dropped me off at my dad's house—and as soon as he answers I realize I don't know what to say to him, not after I've slept with the guys I've slept with, so we just small-talk it for a few minutes and then say goodbye.

Later I go through some boxes in the basement and find my senior yearbook. The first note I read is from this girl in the punk scene who I used to hang out with. She quotes Lou Reed and says maybe I can come party with her if I get bored, and the last thing she writes is, "Don't overdo it on the snow, okay?" I re-read the note a dozen times, wishing there was a "good luck" in there somewhere. I look through my entire yearbook and there's not a single "good luck" scribbled by anyone in my glossy white margins.

I dream about Dale, a guy from college I slept with. In real life he's a modern dancer, and in my dream he's choreographing a dance I'm in, and my tutu is a giant Chicken of the Sea tuna can. It's fucking ridiculous and I can't imagine what it means, but I wake up at 11:30

feeling scared and alone, like I'll be scared and alone forever. The feeling lingers with me throughout the day, an acrid tincture pulsing through my veins.

That afternoon I visit Julie at the new wave clothing store where she works, where we both used to work. We talk about music and clothes and our friends who are doing lots of X, and I ask her about her roommate, Lisa.

"One week she brought home a different guy every night," Julie says like she couldn't be more bored. "She thinks she's pregnant."

"No doubt," I say.

"She has no idea who the father is. She'll just make it whoever she wants it to be."

Julie's got some version of the life I used to have and I honestly can't remember if I was happy. More happened to me in the last three months at college than usually happens in a year, and she's still doing the same as when I left. But am I any better off? The only difference is now I'm more manic than everyone else at my neo-hippie school.

So, I ask Julie, "Are you happy?" thinking she'll make me remember how—who—I was before.

She rests her chin on her hand and says, "Yeah, sure," but she doesn't look happy. She doesn't even look content. I tell her this and she shrugs. "I need a change."

We end the conversation by saying, "Yeah, we'll go dancing Sunday night," and I leave.

When my brother comes home from college that night, he just stares at the way I'm dressed in paisley leggings and a knee-length sweater and a vintage polyester vest and a rosary and gold John Lennon glasses with no lenses and my bleached blonde hair with shaved sides, and he doesn't even try to be discrete about being disgusted. He walks past me and turns a basketball game on TV.

My friends Rebekah and Aaron and I are sitting on my bed listening to The Psychedelic Furs and The Cure and Talking Heads and reading the liner notes, and we're real bored so we decide to get some coke. It's been twenty-nine days since I've done it and I at least wanted to make it to sixty to give myself some sense of accomplishment. I tell myself that just because I do it tonight doesn't mean I'm hooked again, and then I realize that there's no such thing as hooked *again*— hooked is hooked—and that freaks me out. I wonder if the panic shows in my eyes, but Rebekah and Aaron are putting on their coats like everything's fine, because that's how mechanical all this has become for us.

We drive to Leon's new house and Aaron and Rebekah wait in my dad's Cadillac while I run upstairs to Leon's bedroom. He owns a café and has to be at work at five in the morning so he's always in bed early now, not like when we first met, when I had to lobby my mom to change my curfew from midnight to 1 a.m. At first she didn't understand why that one hour made a difference, and it might have been the first time she realized that whatever Leon and I were doing wasn't all bad, but was about comfort and companionship, too.

I hug and kiss Leon and assure him that we'll go out tomorrow night and he gives me a seal and I feel like a coke whore. I tell him I love him but I've got to go because Aaron and Rebekah are waiting in the car. He says, "Yeah, she's probably giving him head by now," and I laugh and run downstairs. As I'm getting in the car, I realize I forgot to lock Leon's door and turn on the alarm, which is super dicey with all that blow lying around.

I start the car and drive away.

Rebekah's sister is in Aspen so we go to her apartment. Rebekah's sister lives alone and has a real job, and wouldn't that be something? To have a real job and a real apartment and a real life, not like when Leon and I were playing house, knowing the entire time that I would leave for college in January, that there was a backdoor out of it all.

I find a big mirror already spotted with coke and an empty Bic pen already caked with coke, and Rebekah's freaking out because she didn't know her sister did coke, and I'm wondering who doesn't? We talk about high school and parties and sex and our friends who've died, and none of that matters as much as the burning in my nose, the burning in my veins, like a live wire let loose. That's the way this shit always goes.

As we're leaving the apartment it's like Aaron finally sees the traces of panic in my eyes and asks, "Are you okay?" but it's already much too late.

We say goodbye in front of my dad's house. Rebekah goes to her car and I kiss Aaron goodnight and he just stands there like he wants more, and I wonder what he expects—for us to do it in his car in front of my dad's house? I tell him that I'll call him, and I walk toward the front door.

The first thing I do is take a shower and tell myself over and over again that what I've done really isn't that bad and I'll be fine, I'll be fine. I lie in bed with all the lights on. I try to remember the last time I was comfortable or content—hell, I'm not even looking for *happy*—and it's so long ago that I can't recall it in my brain or my body. You'd think that would make me sad or at least scared, but it's like I'm in some black hole where love and fear and hope and confusion have collapsed into a heavy, dense mass and nothing can escape. In Portland, I express emotion about every little thing—I sob and I shriek and I shake and do I ever laugh?—and I wonder what it is about Denver that can make me so detached. It must have something to do with the change in altitude.

The red numbers on my clock read 4:07. I always think of morning as starting at 4:30 and that's all I have to do—get to sleep in the next 23 minutes—and then it won't be like I was up all night. I have a sudden craving for orange juice. I think about how Rebekah's gained the Freshman Fifteen, and I can pinch an inch around my hips for the first time in my life, too, and maybe Leon doesn't find me attractive anymore because he's always said it's important that his girlfriend be skinny. I think of the cover of *Purple Rain*, Apollonia in some doorway staring at Prince and he's not even close to staring at her, and that reminds me of the lonely *Petit Prince* and I can't remember if he ever made it home, and I hear a line from Echo and the Bunnymen and I wonder if anyone knows how brittle my little heart really is. I hear my heart pounding and realize there are two separate beatings. One is fast, and the other is a thump, thump, thump. The fast fast is my heart, the thump thump is my head.

I never end up sleeping. I listen to "Why Can't I Have You?" by The Cars over and over. I watch the early morning news and see that Ecstasy has been listed as a Schedule 1 drug, the same as heroin. It's weird that one day a drug is legal and the next day you're a criminal and a junkie for having it. I sit in the steam room and re-read the chapters in *The Prophet* about how death is like standing naked in the sun and the wind, and how love will thresh and grind and crucify you, and I wonder why Gibran didn't make love seem like a much better deal than death.

That afternoon I'm staring through the skylight above my bed and listening to Grace Jones. I think of the last night I spent with Shane in Portland, when he wanted to rub his dick between my breasts until he came and told me not to tell anyone we were seeing each other, and I think of Craig and me fighting one minute and fucking the next and then me crying and making him stop, and I think of Aaron standing outside last night like he wanted something more and the whole idea of sex seems really disgusting to me. And then there's Dale dancing on a stage without me.

It's date night and Leon and I are lying on his bed watching a movie on TV with the sound muted and the *Pretty in Pink* soundtrack on the stereo. The movie stars this girl who was in all the Disney movies when I was a kid. Now she's eighteen or something and is supposed to be real tough and sexy, but I still see her as a little girl with freckles and pigtails. The movie turns out to be super violent so I close my eyes and plug my ears and even start to feel sick to my stomach, but we don't change the channel.

I wonder what the hell I'm going to do about school, about Portland, about this fucking mess that is me. I catch myself thinking, "I wish I would just die," and I know I don't really mean it, so I try to figure out what *do* I mean. I decide that, "I wish things were easy," and I laugh at myself for even thinking something so stupid. I doubt Leon can help me because he's so far past all this, and I wonder if anyone can help. Not too long ago, I thought that person was Dale, but a couple weeks back I told him about the Dean finding out that someone on my floor was dealing and how I wouldn't admit to it and how my R.A. wouldn't turn me in, even though the Dean fired her and kicked her off campus. Dale turned up his nostrils like he smelled rotten meat. "I didn't *ask* her to do that," I said. "She made that decision all on her own." Still, something changed between us after that.

When I leave Leon's house at 1:30, I kiss him goodnight and realize it's the first time our lips have touched all night.

I go home and lie in bed with all the lights on. I can feel the tears welling up, but they never fall, so I sigh—I mean it, I actually *sigh*—and turn off the lights and go to sleep.

When I get to Julie and Lisa's apartment on Sunday night, Julie's not dressed for the club and is drinking a beer. "I got really drunk at a wedding today," she says with a sloppy smile, "and am still trying to mellow out."

Lisa comes out to talk to me and is super friendly and asks me about college. She's wearing tons of makeup and her hair is big and I keep wondering who the father of her baby is.

We do the rest of the coke that Leon gave me, and I don't freak out like I did the other night and I wish there was more. Lisa and Julie are taking forever to get ready so I stand in their dingy kitchen and stare out the window. I'm jealous that they have their own apartment, but seeing them again also makes me think I should go back to school. Because what does this lead to? Where's the end? Where's even the next stop?

I'm jonesing for another couple of lines—that's what's so hard to explain, how something that gets you so wired is something you need so badly to calm you. Over the shitty apartment rooftops is a red neon sign that says JONAS BROS FURS and even though there's nothing spectacular about it I stare at the letters for a really long time, until Julie and Lisa say, "Let's go."

The bar's a big rectangle with a dance floor in the middle and no one's on it when we arrive. We sit down with two girls I used to hang out with, but I can't remember either of their names. Finally, I hear Julie call one of them Jane and I remember the other is Beth and I'm relieved, like my whole life before college might be fake if I didn't get these two chicks' names.

I dance to a couple of songs, then take a break and sit down at the table with Lisa and Beth and Jane. A girl named Heather sits down next to me and Beth asks, "Do you know each other?" We do know each other, but Heather says, "No." So Beth introduces us and I smile and say hi, but Heather just takes a long drag on her cigarette, then throws her head back as she slowly blows out the smoke and finally says, "Hi," in a husky voice. I wonder if the disconnect is about me or about her or is just what happens when this many people swill 3.2 beer near where Kerouac and all those cats used to hang.

Heather leaves after a couple of minutes and Julie sits in her place.

"I feel like I'm really missing something," I say.

"No kidding." Julie nods in agreement.

"I mean, I just don't get it." I don't know exactly what it is I'm supposed to get—I just know I don't.

"I know what you mean," she says, but she really doesn't.

Lisa is yelling, "Fuck you, Robert! You're such a faggot!" to some guy walking by, and I hear myself mutter something about bad karma—a phrase that must have hitchhiked a ride from Oregon—and wonder if Robert's the father of her baby.

Finally we leave the bar and go back to Julie's apartment. As I'm getting my purse out of her room, I see a carved wooden sign amid all the pictures of when Julie used to do ballet, when she was thin and didn't smoke or do coke. The sign says, **Dancers Do It With Rhythm**, and it makes me choke on my bitter spit. I leave the room fast.

The next day I drop by Benetton to see Dennis. He's wearing black stirrup pants and a long yellow sweater and his hair is gelled back into a ponytail. He looks a little bit femme, but his shirt is unbuttoned so you can see some of his chest and he has a really nice chest, so he doesn't look too femme. Dennis seems really happy to see me and he wants to know if I went to The Alarm last night, and I tell him no, I'm not into The Alarm, and he assures me I would have been after last night.

We talk about concerts and the new Depeche Mode album and drugs, and I tell him that X is now a Schedule 1 drug. This kind of freaks him out because he's getting $100 worth of X to sell on Friday night, but he shrugs it off, it'll be fine. He asks me if I'm still going out with "that guy" and I tell him it depends on your point of view.

He leans back in his chair and smiles, like the whole idea of me and Leon having problems is delicious. "Oh yeah? How is your steady beau?" "Not so steady," I say, and the phone rings. It's some high school girl who has a crush on Dennis. He has absolutely no idea who she is but plays with her mind for a while and tells her maybe she can take him out to dinner sometime. He hangs up and says, "Weird."

I go to the bank with him to make the store deposit, and it turns out we have the same sunglasses, and then we figure out we bought the same jacket at Fashion Disaster last week. After we get back from the bank, he says, "Good luck at school," and it was really good seeing me and we'll get together when I'm home for the summer, and I know we won't, we won't ever see or talk to each other ever again.

I go home to watch *Dallas* re-runs on my dad's gigantic TV, but there's a special news report on instead. Libyan and American forces have been shooting at each other since eleven o'clock this morning, and we're now in the process of sinking one of their ships, but some government suit says, "We are *not* in a war." I'm really scared and I want to talk to someone, but none of my friends in Denver would understand why it matters that people are being shot and killed halfway around the world.

I call my mom and we talk about Libya, even though I want to talk about everything else, but if she doesn't approve of Leon she sure isn't going to approve of all the guys and sex and my first ever "D" and the dealing coke disaster and the bloody noses I got after I quit. Finally, *Dallas* comes back on and I can turn off the fear. Or mute it, at least.

I call Rebekah, who's back at college in Missouri—or Misery, as she calls it—and ask her if I should break up with Leon. I love him, but I don't know if it's long-haul love, the kind that survives me being in college and sleeping with guys Leon doesn't know about. Rebekah says if I really feel that way, I should probably do it.

"Do you think he'll take it bad?" she asks.

"I don't think he's expecting it at all," I say.

I go over to Leon's house that night and he lays his head in my lap and looks like a defenseless puppy, and I know I won't be able to do it. As I'm tucking him into bed, I ask, "Am I still your best friend?"

He thinks about it a little too long, then says, "Well, you're one of my best friends."

"How come I'm not your best friend anymore?"

"I don't think we're as close anymore. It's like we already went through all that." He shrugs.

"Will we still be friends no matter what happens?" I ask.

"Of course."

I kiss him goodnight and he says, "I love you," and I just smile so he asks, "Do you love me?"

"Of course," I answer. "You're my best friend."

He looks worried, but I don't say anything to reassure him, just "Talk to you later," and I leave. This time I remember to lock the door and set the alarm.

The next day I just talk to Leon on the phone. He tells me that he saw Josh—who sends his love—and the reason why we haven't seen Josh in so long is because he just got out of rehab. I can't believe it since Josh is one of the biggest hoover-heads we know. He always owes Leon money, and since his dad is a big jazz promoter, he used to take us to these concerts where we'd sit third-row center and go backstage during intermission and do blow with famous sax and trumpet players, and afterwards go to El Chapultepec and do more blow with them. The one who always sticks in my head is the one who politely told me, "I don't need that stuff" when I offered him a line.

Leon tells me Josh has color in his cheeks for the first time since we met him, and he's gained twenty-six pounds. "Now he's on his way to a halfway house in Arizona."

"How did you see him?" I ask.

"He called me to buy an eight-ball," Leon says. I don't ask if he sold it to him because I don't want to think about what it would mean if he did.

Leon tells me that he's going dancing with some friends that night, but he's got a card for me that he'll drop off on his way. I'm anxious to see the card—even a little hopeful that it'll say something to make it clear what we're supposed to do with our relationship, but Leon and that card never stop by.

I call Leon the next day. "What happened to my card?"

"I changed my mind," he says. "It's too mushy and sentimental."

"Since when does that matter?"

"I don't know," Leon says, and he sounds like he's talking into the phone from the other side of the room. "I just didn't want you and your mom sitting around laughing at me."

I slam down the phone … and the thing is, I want to call my mom. We used to be great friends and we'd talk about blow jobs and smoking pot and what it means to be a woman. That's probably why she got so distant—not because of anything to do with Leon, but because I stopped talking to her about everything.

Leon calls me back. "Why did you hang up on me?"

"I can't even believe you think I'd laugh at your feelings," I say. "That's so insulting."

"I'm just insecure about our relationship." His voice is close now, not across the room. "If we have a relationship anymore."

"You don't understand," I whisper.

"Understand what?"

"That I have as much to lose as you."

We don't say anything else right then and there, but we both know it's over. It's just that neither of us have the guts—or the heart—to pull the trigger.

I make a mixtape for Leon that I drop off at his work. On the cover I write a line from an OMD song, a line about how we'll always be friends, or meet again, or something like that, someday.

When I get to Leon's house he's listening to the tape. We listen together for a while without saying anything, and towards the end he starts crying. Not just teary eyes, but real sobbing, and I think I've never seen anything like it in my entire life, and it makes me cry, too. We cry for a while, then we eat frozen Chinese dinners, and then I tell him I don't love him anymore and he says he doesn't love me either. We watch some TV and I go home.

And after two years, Leon and I are broken up.

Thursday is sunny so I lie out in the backyard. My brother is digging a hole for some reason, and when he finally notices me on the grass, he asks, "Are you trying to get a tan?"

"Not necessarily," I say. "I'm just trying to look less dead."

He doesn't get it.

I tell him he would if he lived in Portland, and he asks me why I stay there if I don't like it. I tell him I've been trying to figure that out for the last three months of my life.

Later, Julie and I drive around listening to Cabaret Voltaire. She says that Scott had to have his stomach pumped and has been in the hospital all week because he did ten hits of X on Saturday night. She thinks he's fucking up his life and I'm like, "Well, sure," and she says, "No, it's not just the drugs and the booze, he's sleeping around a lot, too. On Saturday night, he fucked Omar."

"Everyone fucks Omar," I say.

"And Mark at the same time."

"Christ." It's not like Scott doesn't have a girlfriend and I wonder if she was there, too. "Does Lisa still think she's pregnant?"

"She hasn't had a period for a couple of months," Julie says.

"Hasn't she seen a doctor yet?"

"No. Who knows, she could be too far along for an abortion now."

I wonder why Julie, as Lisa's best friend, doesn't maybe tell her this. When Julie drops me off in front of my dad's house, she asks, "Are you going dancing tonight?"

"I don't know." I adjust my sunglasses against the mile-high sun. "I still don't get it."

"Yeah, I know," she says. "So, I'll see you there."

When I get to the bar it's packed with girls wearing denim mini-skirts and guys in cowboy boots. I ask Lisa and Julie what's going on, and they're all glum. "College kids. Spring break." It makes sense for a second, but then I remember no one at my college dresses this way.

When Beth shows up she quickly lights a cigarette and says, "I'm in the worst mood."

"I've never seen you in a bad mood before," I say.

"Yeah, well my cousin was murdered a couple of months ago, and we just found out that the guy who did it got off with a light sentence. Hiya' hon," she says and squeezes the arm of the pretty boy next to her. "Anyway," she says to me, "I'm not exactly sure why I'm here."

I nod my head slowly. "Yeah, I can see that."

By eleven o'clock I'm more bored than I've ever been and decide to leave. All at the same time, some guy asks me to dance and Julie asks me if I want to go thrift shopping the next day and the guy sitting behind her smiles at me. I tell Julie yes, even though I mean no, and I look over the head of the guy smiling at me and tell the other one I'm leaving and I don't think he understands.

I sit in my dad's Cadillac for a long time and stare at the bright lights and tall buildings and the forgotten railroad tracks and Kerouac's ghost, and realize I will die if I don't get the hell away from this city. I start the car and leave downtown behind.

On Friday afternoon I'm sitting at a table outside Leon's café when Todd walks by with a really feminine haircut and too much makeup, and some guy I've never seen before. I ask Todd where he's working and where he's living these days.

He waves a hand. "Work? What work? I haven't worked in ages." I wonder how he's paying his bills and if the rumors are true that he's tricking at Cheesman Park. "But I'm living in this *great* house in Capitol Hill. With Mark."

I want to ask him if it's true that Mark and Scott and Omar slept together, but I don't know the guy that's with him so I just ask, "Did you know Scott's in the hospital?"

"Yeah, he got out last night. I didn't know you know Scott. Do you also know—"

"Omar. Yeah, we know each other."

"Well, that's my Saturday Night X Club," Todd says, remotely excited.

"You guys are still doing that?" I ask.

"Sure, why not?" he says, and it's about the hundredth time I wonder if I'm the one missing something.

Todd sucks on his cigarette and looks around. "I can't believe I've lived in Denver for a year now. And what have I done?" he asks. "Five different jobs, five different apartments, and five different hair colors." He laughs. "And lots of drugs."

Despite all the make-up, he's still shit-ass pale and thin.

"So, what are you doing here?" Todd asks. "I heard you two broke up." He motions towards Leon's café.

"Where did you hear that?" I ask, wondering if news could really spread that fast.

"Didn't *you* tell me? No?" He thinks a minute. "Oh, I know. I saw you with another guy. No, wait. I saw him with another girl. Oh, I don't know," he waves a hand. "Maybe I just heard it somewhere. I always thought he was too old for you anyway."

"Well, we only broke up two days ago," I say.

"Really? Hmm." He pauses. "Well, I'm so *hot* I'm absolutely going to *die*. We've got to get out of this sun."

"Besides, it'll give you wrinkles when you're older," I say.

"Oh, who cares? As soon as I turn twenty-five I'm committing suicide anyway," Todd says and I believe him. He hugs me and says, "Ciao, baby," then jumps in a white convertible Cabriolet with the other guy. They turn on some dance song—real loud—and wave as they speed west.

My plane sits on the runway for thirty-seven minutes before take-off. Soon I will be back at college, and I'm not scared or anxious or lonely or jumping out of my skin. In a week I will move to the hippie dorm, where nobody even thinks of coke, where they smoke pot and drop acid and play acoustic guitar and give each other backrubs on threadbare sofas.

Dale will transfer to art school in San Francisco, but won't tell me he's leaving; someone else will tell me and we will say goodbye only minutes before he drives away with a U-Haul hitched to the back of his car. A year later we will end up sitting next to each other on a bench in Union Square, but neither of us will acknowledge the other and he will eventually just walk away.

Leon will get a new girlfriend right away. He will propose to her and she will tell him he's not allowed to be friends with me, so he will burn all his pictures of me and throw away my letters. She will get pregnant and have an abortion and break up with him six months after they met. Two men will ambush Leon on his front lawn and hold him at gunpoint and steal his money and drugs and shoot his dog. Leon will never deal or do coke again. He will get married and I will go to his wedding, and a few years later he will go to mine. He will have two sons and get divorced, and when my entire family dies twenty-five years after Leon and I broke up, he will help me clean out my dad's house before it goes into foreclosure.

Rebekah will get married surrounded by hundreds of sterling roses, and she will raise two funny and generous daughters. One day we will sit on the stairs of my dad's house and she will help me encase my dad and brother's urns in bubble wrap to ship from Denver to Portland, where my husband and I live.

My mom's ashes are already sprinkled in Half-Moon Bay.

Julie will marry a guy she barely knows. He will hit her and hit her and hit her, until one day their daughter pleads, "Please don't kill mommy!" so Julie will leave him and finally marry someone kind.

Todd will die of AIDS.

I watch the sun sink behind the Rocky Mountains, turning the sky orange and pink and magenta red and I think it's the most beautiful sunset I've ever seen. My plane finally takes off and I wonder if we'll crash into the Continental Divide. As we climb higher into the stratus altocumulus cirrocumulus, I feel like crying, but I can't, I can't for days—for weeks—afterward, and I never really know why. Maybe it's the change in altitude.

Scenes From My Youth

1976: An American Underdog Story

This is the scene in *Rocky* where Rocky walks Adrian to his place after their sweet first date at the ice rink, where he paid the Zamboni driver ten bucks to let them skate for ten minutes. It's late at night, and the streets are empty. Standing outside his apartment, Rocky brags that in all his years of boxing, no one has ever broken his nose. Lots of guys threw punches and slapped at him, he says, and mimes a punch towards Adrian. She flinches.

Rocky tries to get Adrian to come inside his apartment. She says no. He wants to show her these exotic animals he has (turtles that she sold him from the pet shop where she works). Adrian says no. Rocky says he has to go to the bathroom (it's a base need she's depriving him of, see?) and she still says no. Adrian tells him she has to go. He asks her if his is a face she can trust, but it's not really a question, it's a statement: Okay, so I beat guys up for the mob for a living when I'm not beating guys up in the ring, but you can trust me.

Trust me.

Rocky walks into his apartment, leaving Adrian on the sidewalk in a really shitty part of North Philly. So, she follows him. Once inside his messy one-room apartment, Rocky takes off his sweater, revealing his beefy musculature. Adrian stands awkwardly by the mattress Rocky uses for a punching bag, stuffing bursting from its battered seams. He tells Adrian to come sit on the couch next to him, but she doesn't. He tells her two more times. He tells her to relax.

This would all be easier if you'd just relax.

Adrian says she wants to call her brother and tell him where she is. Rocky yells out the window, "Yo, Paulie! Your sister's with me!" Ha, ha, you want to call your brother, see what I just did? He walks towards Adrian and grabs onto an exposed pipe overhead, so he's literarily looming over her. He asks her what the problem is. Doesn't she like him?

Don't you like me?

Adrian tells him twice that she doesn't feel comfortable. Adrian also twice says that she doesn't know him well enough to be alone with him in his apartment. Adrian tells Rocky she doesn't feel comfortable and has to go. She walks to the door, and Rocky puts one hand on the door, one hand on the wall, trapping Adrian in the corner. Rocky asks Adrian to do him a favor and take off her glasses. He doesn't let her decide for herself if that's what she wants and removes them from her face. He tells her she has nice eyes. He wants her to do him another favor, to take off her wool cap. He strips it from her. "I always knew you was pretty," he says.

You know, if you'd just let him remake you.

Rocky tells Adrian he wants to kiss her. He tells her she doesn't have to kiss him back, but he's going to kiss her. Adrian really has no choice in the matter, since the only way out of that corner is through Rocky's muscles.

Listen, I don't care if you enjoy this or even want it—you can just be still—but it's what I want.

Rocky kisses Adrian and she doesn't kiss back at first. Then she gives in, the passion takes over, and they slump to the floor of Rocky's shitty apartment, where they presumably have sex.

The next time we see them together, Adrian is giddy that Rocky called her his girlfriend on TV. Adrian marries Rocky, almost dies having his baby, stands by him through every dangerous boxing match he endures, and ultimately she dies of cancer, an angel. A martyr.

1979: A Fairy Tale Romance

This is the scene on *General Hospital* when Luke and Laura are alone in the Campus Disco after it has closed. Luke works for a local mobster who has ordered him to kill a dangerous rival. Luke knows if he does it, he'll be a marked man. But if he doesn't, his own boss will rub him out. He tells Laura he loves her, that she's all he ever thinks about. Laura is married to Scotty Baldwin and tells Luke she doesn't want anyone but Scotty. Luke tells her it tears him up inside, imagining her sleeping in the same bed as her husband.

Laura tells Luke she only sees him as a friend. He drops the needle on a Herb Alpert record. Horns moan, red and blue colored lights flash from the periphery, the music and lights merging into one. Luke tells Laura he doesn't want to be her friend. "Look what you've done to me!" he yells.

It's Laura's fault, this state he's in—drunk, scared, impassioned and angry.

Luke says he can't die without holding her and tells her to dance with him. Laura says no. He repeats his command, grabbing Laura's hand and pulling her towards him. Laura tells him she has to go. He pushes his lips into her neck. Laura asks him to let her call a taxi, please. Laura tells Luke he's frightening her. She again says no.

Luke grabs Laura's wrists and kisses her hard. Laura says, "No! Let me go!" He pulls Laura to the floor. She says NO.
NO.
NO.

The camera twirls around the disco, landing on the colored lights mounted in the corner, the only witnesses to what is happening on the floor. Then the camera pans away from the lights, and back to Luke. He's standing above Laura, his shirt unbuttoned. Laura is curled up in a ball on the floor crying. Her clothes ripped. Laura runs out the door. Luke picks up her abandoned sweater from the floor. "Oh my god," he says. "What have I done?" Luke falls to his knees and cries.

Within six months, Laura realizes she's in love with Luke. She writes him a letter telling him so, and, to make a really long story short, they run away together and have all sorts of crazy, romantic adventures. Luke and Laura become daytime soap's first super couple, sending *General Hospital's* ratings soaring. In November of 1981, they married in an elaborate outdoor wedding watched by thirty million viewers. "The Ultimate TV Wedding," it was called. "A Fairy Tale." When Anthony Geary, who played Luke, arrived at fan events, women carried signs and wore T-shirts saying, "Rape me, Luke!" They shouted it after him. They walked up to him on the street. One woman after another.

Rape me, Luke, rape me.

1979: An Irreverent Misfit Comedy

This is the scene in *Meatballs* where Tripper (played by Bill Murry) and Roxanne (Kate Lynch) are working on the camp activity schedule alone in a cabin. Tripper comes up behind Roxanne and looks down her blouse, telling her he can see everything. She moves away quickly and asks what's wrong with him. He makes a deadpan joke that falls, well, dead. Then Tripper says, "Let's wrestle!"

Roxanne says, "Let's not, okay, Tripper?" He lunges towards her. Roxanne tries to run away. He grabs her from behind, pinning her arms against her body. In self-defense class, women learn to counteract this move by punching their elbows into the man's torso or kicking backwards into his shin. This is what we're taught to do when a stranger attacks us when we're alone at night. Roxanne says, "Let's not do this," and "Let's stop right now," each time adding on "Okay?" or "All right?"—as if she's asking, not telling.

Tripper continues to leap and lurch, Roxanne continues to duck and run. Tripper suddenly falls to the floor, and Roxanne looks momentarily confused. He's thrown her off her guard by playing possum. He jumps up and grabs Roxanne around the waist. Tripper plops down on the couch, throwing Roxanne face down on his lap like he's going to spank her. She yells NO. She says, "Don't do that!" Roxanne struggles to escape, trying to crawl onto the floor. This particular position wasn't covered in self-defense class. Prone and pinned, your movements are limited. She yells NO.
NO.
NO.

Tripper throws her on her back and climbs on top of her. She holds her hands against his chest and again says, "Let's stop, okay?"

Roxanne has now said some version of "no" or "stop" nine times in thirty-five seconds.

Roxanne tells Tripper to get off her immediately or she'll start screaming. Tripper doesn't get off, so Roxanne screams for help. He screams to cover up Roxanne's screams. Tripper rolls onto the floor and pulls Roxanne on top of him and starts yelling for help. Morty, the camp director, walks in wanting to know what the hell is going on. Tripper pushes Roxanne off of him, and runs to Morty, pretending to cry. He sobs and wails that Roxanne attacked him. Morty realizes this is ridiculous, yet also seems unaware of or unconcerned for Roxanne's safety.

The next time we see Tripper and Roxanne is at the camp dance. Tripper interrupts a conversation Roxanne and Morty are having, telling Morty he needs to talk to her alone. He pulls her onto the dance floor without asking. Roxanne doesn't push him away or say no, and participates in the dancing. They are doing the same dance moves as Luke and Laura. He pulls her close to his chest. He twirls her out, he pulls her back in again. They exchange some Hepburn and Tracey-like banter, but with the clever factor of seventh graders. Then Tripper says, "Three years of this … I don't think I have many lines left."

He's been doing this for three years. Three summers in a row.

Tripper suggest they go outside and get some air, and Roxanne says no. He stops dancing and stands a respectable distance away from her. In a voice that's the closest thing Bill Murray can come to sincerity, Tripper says, "Well, I'm tryin'." Roxanne pauses, evaluates his lone moment of vulnerability. "So, keep trying," she says.

Keep it up, some day I will finally give in.

The next time we see Tripper and Roxanne together they have sex under the stars during a campout, and skinny dip in the lake by moonlight. By the end of the movie, they've decided to move in together. All Tripper had to do to get the girl was try harder. He just had to keep pushing, long after she'd said no, no, no.

1983: A Comedy for and About Teens

This is the scene in *Sixteen Candles* when the perfect guy, the dreamboat, Jake, decides he's over his blond, blue-eyed party girl girlfriend, Caroline. Jake is the perfect guy: he's impossibly handsome, his parents are Rolls Royce-rich, he throws bitchin' parties, and he's deep. We know Jake is deep because as soon as he learns that freckled, not-popular sophomore, Samantha, has a crush on him, he wants her. He sees she has substance, and spends an entire bitchin' party at his parents' house trying to find her.

But Jake must get rid of Caroline so he can pursue Sam. By the end of the party Caroline is totally smashed, so he hands her off to a character called The Geek. The Geek could never get a girl like Caroline, not on his own, not if she was sober, so Jake magnanimously tells The Geek to take her home and do what he wants with her. "She's so blitzed she won't know the difference," he says. "Have fun." Jake even lends The Geek his parents' Rolls Royce.

The next morning when Caroline regains consciousness in the Rolls Royce, The Geek asks her if they had sex. We're not sure why he's not sure, because at no point were we led to believe he was blackout smashed. He was able to drive, after all. They decide they did have sex, and he asks Caroline if she enjoyed it. "You know," Caroline says, smiling, "I have this weird feeling I did."

It turns out the perfect guy did Caroline a favor, giving her blackout sex with a stranger.

1985: Young Adult Dramady

This is the scene in *St. Elmo's Fire* where Bad Boy Billy (played by sexy Rob Lowe) and Bad Girl Jules (played by sexy Demi Moore) are in her Jeep outside of the house he shares with his baby mama. It's late at night and Billy's had too much to drink. The two flirt a little— it's obvious they slept together sometime during their recent college years—and they kiss in the Jeep. But Jules says, "Enough."

"Says who?" Billy asks. Jules asserts that *she* says. He mocks her that she has any authority to decide when to stop. Jules reiterates that she has this right. Billy suggests that she wouldn't be able to say no if his cock was in her mouth. He thinks he's being cute, seductive, irresistible, the idea that he could take away her ability to say no.

Jules says NO again and tells him she's serious. Billy grabs her keys out of the ignition and puts them down his pants. Jules demands them back, but he informs her she'll have to come and get them. Jules hits him, grabs him, kicks him out of her Jeep so he's on the cold, wet ground. And then she tells him with tears, "You break my heart."

This experience is never mentioned again and, in the end, Billy is the one who saves Jules from her nervous breakdown. She's lost her job, all her furniture has been re-possessed, and the stepmother Jules thought she hated has died, and Jules suddenly realizes she cares. She's shivering in her locked apartment with all the windows open, when Billy comes to her rescue. He tells Jules what she's experiencing, what she's feeling, isn't *real*. This is all an illusion, he convinces her. Bad Boy Billy is the one who saves Bad Girl Jules from herself.

Real Life

This is the scene sometime—anytime—in the 1980s, when a boy and a girl, a young man and a young woman who know each other are alone together. He makes a move she doesn't want him to make, and she says no. She says stop. She's says I'm not comfortable. She says let me go. What does he hear when she says these words? What does he picture? Does he picture a triumphant underdog, a soap opera hero, an irreverent jokester, the perfect guy, the sexy bad boy who saves the girl in the end? Does he see sex or power or violation or love or a woman crying on the floor?

This is the scene the next day—and for years afterwards—when the girl, the young woman, the grown woman wonders "What happened that night?" He was a friend—wasn't he? He was a good guy, right? I mean, everyone likes him. Maybe there's something wrong with me. Maybe I gave him mixed signals. Maybe I didn't say NO strong enough, often enough, loud enough. Maybe it was my fault. Maybe I take things too seriously. Maybe … it was no big deal.

That Long, Weird Essay That's Entirely About Beverly Hills, 90210

Once upon a not-so-distant time ago, there were no nighttime TV dramas for and about teenagers. There was no *Riverdale* or *Gossip Girl*, no *Veronica Mars*, *Buffy the Vampire Slayer*, or even *Dawson's Creek*. But in 1990, Aaron Spelling, the producer behind the eighties megahit *Dynasty*, took a chance on a wild idea: a nighttime soap about teens. They weren't just any teens, though; they lived in one of America's richest and ritziest zip codes, *Beverly Hills, 90210*.

The original premise of *Beverly Hills, 90210* followed recently relocated mid-westerners Brandon and Brenda Walsh as they tried to fit in with their new rich and pretty friends in Beverly Hills. During its ten-year run, *90210* tackled plots that ranged from cheating on tests to first love, sex, race, addiction, partner abuse, rape, and a lot of stupid stuff I don't want to get into. I was twenty-three when *Beverly Hills, 90210* premiered and twenty-four when I actually started watching it—not only out of high school, but also out of college, and presumably not the target audience. But I *was*. Because I was Generation X, the same generation who was mesmerized by the gloss of MTV for the first time, the same generation who obsessed over "Who Shot J.R.?," the same generation weaned on *General Hospital*. That was the magic of *90210*; it appealed to teens experiencing real-life issues in real time, and the young adults who wished there had been TV like this for us during our recent, not-so-halcyon days.

Teen issues being dealt with so realistically was new to network TV. *The Wonder Years* (1988-1993) was a teen drama, but told in retrospect through an adult voice looking back on the sixties. It was very much a show for and about Baby Boomers. The Canadian *Degrassi* series had broken ground as a realistic teen drama, but it only aired on select PBS stations in the U.S. (An internet rumor posits that Spelling unsuccessfully tried to buy the U.S. rights to the series, but the Exec Producer of *Degrassi* says no, that never happened.) American Gen Xers had mostly been fed a diet of ridiculously earnest *Afterschool Specials* with titles like "All the Kids Do It" and "Reading, Writing, and Reefer," or the Very Special Episode phenomenon on select sitcoms (Arnold is targeted by a pedophile on *Diff'rent Strokes*; Mallory's "uncle" gets handsy with her on *Family Ties*; Blair considers losing her virginity on *Facts of Life*).

But when you've grown up latchkey during the Iran Hostage Crisis, and listened on your transistor radio when John Lennon was assassinated, and AIDS explodes just as you're discovering your sexuality, that level of earnest doesn't work anymore. Shit doesn't get solved just because someone makes the right choice, the *moral* choice. Yet, there was still some way Gen X need and wanted the fantasy of a moral universe. Despite the financial crisis of the late eighties (and the morality play of Oliver Stone's *Wall Street*), we were still captivated by the aspirational lifestyles of the rich and famous, by the (mostly) privileged teens of John Hughes movies, and the eternal youth of MTV. *Beverly Hills, 90210* fused all these concepts in a glossy depiction of the lives of American teenagers.

The Class of Beverly Hills

Most viewers referred to the original series by its zip code alone: *90210*. But then a remake called *90210* (*sans* "Beverly Hills" and with a new cast) aired from 2008-2013, throwing some confusion in the nomenclature mix. In 2019, a super meta reboot called *BH90210* aired six episodes, further blurring what to call what. I'm a purist (holy shit, I just said that about this show), and will refer to the original series as *90210*. I swear, I will not be talking about the 2008 remake, which somehow managed to feature even worse acting than the final years of the original series.

The Back Story

Beverly Hills, 90210 ran on Fox from 1990-2000. Although Fox billed itself as "the fourth network," in 1990, it was mostly a conglomeration of small UHF channels that agreed to air Fox's scant nighttime programming. Then Fox made an incredibly shrewd move: in September 1990, it struck a deal with Tele-Communications Inc. (TCI), the country's largest owner of cable TV systems, to allow certain TCI franchises to become Fox affiliates. It gave Fox an unprecedented reach into rural areas where there were no local UHF stations to adopt Fox programming. TCI also agreed to move the Fox signal to Channel 13 or below on its cable systems in order to boost viewing. A month later, *90210* debuted.

Although *90210* aired for a decade, I'm going to ignore the majority of the last two to three (or three to four) seasons because they are so terrible all I could possibly do is rant about the dreadful acting and asinine storylines (here's a hint: someone gets amnesia and someone else comes back from the dead). *90210* succeeded when it focused on kids in high school (and maybe a couple of the college years?). It all went to hell when they started straining for soapy storylines, but without the screaming camp of *Melrose Place*.

When the show premiered, the majority of "The Gang" were sixteen-year-old juniors, with the exception of freshman David Silver. All of them white. At the end of season one, The Gang finished the school year, had a fun and fraught summer vacation, and then fretted about starting school again (depicted through a montage of deciding what to wear on the first day). But wait! They're inexplicably still juniors. Or they're juniors again. But somehow David Silver had been promoted to a sophomore, and by the time they all graduate at the end of season three, he's taken enough extra credits to graduate, too. The two consecutive junior years is a widely acknowledged—but unexplained—phenomenon of the *90210* world, the opposite of rapid soap opera aging syndrome, when child characters suddenly become teens to inhabit juicy storylines.

Friends, Lovers, and Children

The main cast was relatively stable for the first four seasons, constituting what is referred to as "The Gang." Brenda (played by Shannen Doherty) and Brandon (Jason Priestley) are teen twins living with their wholesome parents, Jim and Cindy Walsh. Brenda is immediately befriended by Kelly Taylor (Jennie Garth), who just got a nose job and drives a BMW. Her ex is spoiled and snotty Steve Sanders (Ian Ziering), who inexplicably decides that not-super-rich, not-yet-popular, drives-a-hunk-of-junk-car Brandon is his new best friend. Brandon is also befriended by mysterious bad boy Dylan McKay (Luke Perry), who drives a Porsche Roadster and has sideburns and quotes poetry and, in case you didn't get it, is supposed to evoke James Dean. Andrea Zuckerman (Gabrielle Carteris) is the high-achieving, overly intense editor of the school newspaper—who dresses like a thirty-year-old office worker—and nurses a crush on Brandon for fucking forever. Geeky David Silver (Brian Austin Green) is constantly trying to weasel his way into The Gang, including a borderline stalker obsession with Kelly. Donna Martin (Tori Spelling) doesn't have much of a role during season one and isn't the same character as she is from season two on—a sweet and slightly ditzy virgin who rarely does anything wrong—and becomes involved with David during her second junior year/his sophomore year. Although Valerie Malone (Tiffani Thiessen) doesn't join the cast until season five, she gets mentioned in this Long Weird Essay because she brought a lot of intimate pathos to the show (when the writers let her just be complex, and not inexplicably evil in the way that made you think Val watched too many soap operas, herself). The Gang all hangs out at the Peach Pit, or works at the Peach Pit, or owns part of the Peach Pit—a diner run by middle-aged Nat (Joe E. Tata), who appears to have no friends his own age.

Rock of Ages

I resolutely believe that if anyone under the age of forty watches *90210* in repeats, at least half the reason they won't get the show is because it doesn't contain its original soundtrack. The licensing rights for songs originally used in the series expired and were too expensive to renew—or something like that—and were junked in later syndication and DVDs. I never realized how significant the music was in adding emotional heft to the show until it was gone. A few examples:

> • When homeless Dylan is shivering in a beach cabana remembering how his felon father once promised to take care of him forever, R.E.M.'s deeply poetic "You Are the Everything" originally plays over Dylan's melancholic memories.

- "Go!" by Tones on Tail plays while Emily buys the U4EA she slips into Brandon's drink at an underground club, adding an alternative coolness to the scene that explains why The Gang is so uncomfortable there.

- When Dylan and Kelly realize they have feelings for each other, Sophie B. Hawkins' "Damn, I Wish I Was Your Lover" plays the episode out as the two cuddle under a beach blanket in front of a fire, under shooting stars.

But because of the licensing snafu, those emotionally resonant songs have been replaced by bland nineties rock, fifties standards, or just stripped out entirely. Not only entire scenes, but entire EPISODES have been removed from syndication because they couldn't eliminate or overdub the music effectively. It turns out that purging Elvis Costello, Depeche Mode, Erasure, Concrete Blonde, The Replacements, Pet Shop Boys, and The Kinks seriously alters the entire aesthetic and removes a level of cool this otherwise mainstream drama needed.

Scared Very Straight

I'm going to quickly dispense with the drinking and drugs aspects of the series, because it was usually so unrealistic in these storylines that they don't deserve much space. In the world of *90210*, drinking and drugs are always wrong. Characters who get drunk inevitably crash their car or hit someone with their car, get expelled from school, end up accused of date rape or are a victim of date rape. Moderate use is an oxymoron. Several characters became full-on addicts after only a few weeks of drug use (Kelly: cocaine, David: meth, Donna: pain killers). A side character who's a pothead even dies of a heroin overdose—because that's what happens, kids, if you smoke reefer!

I so often wonder how Baby Boomers were writing this nonsense, and how the Gen X actors weren't saying, "Seriously, man? Have you really never met people our age?" I'm not saying all young people drink and do drugs, but enough do that it's unrealistic and stupid to portray it in such black and white terms.

Dylan McKay was the only character whose substance abuse storyline came remotely close to realistic. He was a recovering alcoholic and drug addict who relapsed several times. His addiction wasn't just a plot to bump ratings during sweeps, but was his entire character arc. Unfortunately, the last years of *90210* took his addiction to a ridiculous extreme, sidestepping reality at numerous points (like, he can suddenly drink without going off the rails? When he's on heroin he has the manic energy of a meth head?), but pretty much everything went off the rails in those last two years, and I promised I wouldn't rant about it. So, let's move on to the important issues at hand.

Who's Zoomin' Who?

90210 was fueled by sex. It was a soapy drama, after all, populated with young pretty people. But the girls were almost always given the misogynistic short shrift when it came to their sexual behavior. Brandon losing his virginity to his visiting Minnesota girlfriend in season one, for instance, is barely a problem. Cindy (Mama Walsh) worries that since the girl is their houseguest, they have a responsibility to her parents to protect her virtue. Ultimately, Jim and Cindy decide what's important is whether or not Brandon was responsible and used protection (he did). For the rest of high school, Brandon's sex life—the fact that he has an active sex life—is a given.

When Brenda lost her virginity six months later, the world apparently lost their fucking minds. Darren Star, the head writer and creator of the show, said that network affiliates were furious that a teen girl had sex and enjoyed it. Never mind that it was with someone she loved, and they were in an expensive hotel room dressed pretty, and they used protection. Star said the affiliates demanded Brenda have negative consequences, and it was strongly suggested he write a storyline addressing that. So, at the end of the next episode (the season one finale) she tells Dylan her period is late.

The cliffhanger isn't resolved for two months, when the show launches its second season. Brenda takes a home pregnancy test which is inconclusive. She goes to an OB/GYN and gets her period while there. Unfortunately, Cindy finds the home pregnancy test in the trash, and Brenda's parents confront her. They tell her that just because she's physically ready for sex doesn't mean she's emotionally ready. Brenda asserts she is, and Cindy says, "I just wonder if five years from now you're going to look back and think the same thing." By the end of the episode, this whole pregnancy scare has made Brenda aware that she's "just not ready for a sexual relationship," so she breaks up with Dylan entirely.

But that line when Brenda tells Dylan she might be pregnant? It aired one week after the episode where she loses her virginity. When did affiliates have time to throw a hissy fit, *and* for the show to be re-written? And let's say I believe that the pressure came from the "affiliates," and not from, say, old dude Aaron Spelling. It still leaves us with the very obvious conclusion that Brandon never suffers negative consequences for his sex life. No one ever tells *him* that he might not be emotionally ready and regret *his* decision years later.

This double standard continues throughout the entire run of the show: nearly every woman frets about losing her virginity, or possibly being pregnant/whether to get an abortion/having had an abortion, maybe having contracted HIV, or being seen as a slut. The guys do not.

Valerie Malone is the character most often branded a slut. She moves in with the Walsh family in season five (1995), after her father kills himself and her mother is too distraught to care for her. This makes Val sound like a toddler who needs her shoes tied and supervision when using the stove, when, in fact, she is already in college. But Val is looking for an escape from her dysfunctional family in Buffalo, and moves into Brenda's room.

Val was on the show until mid-1998, and in that time sleeps with Steve, Dylan, David, Noah, Collin, Ray, and hooks up with, but doesn't sleep with, Brandon. She also beds an up-and-coming actor who I want to call Smith because he's played by the same guy who played Samantha's up-and-coming actor boyfriend on *Sex and the City*, a married man, an FBI agent, her mother's fiancé (ew!), a random heroin addict, and her old friend, Tom. Tom ushered in a new piece of Valerie's backstory when he arrived in 1997: he was the only person who knew Val's father had molested her.

Violated

90210 tackled plots about rape in many forms: Brenda talking to a cheerleader raped by the football players she cheers for; Kelly revealing that her first sex was wham bam never-talk-to-you-again; Kelly being attacked at a Halloween party when she's dressed provocatively; the new roguishly handsome English teacher being accused of sexual impropriety by a student who is actually being molested by her uncle; Steve having a one-night stand with a woman who later accuses him of date rape; Donna being attacked by a serial rapist in her apartment and saved by David; Valerie being sexually harassed by a professor who turns out to be a serial predator; Valerie revealing that her father repeatedly molested her; Valerie waking up to realize she'd been drugged and had intercourse with Noah and charges him with rape; David being arrested for statutory rape; and, finally, Kelly being raped at knifepoint by a stranger in an alley.

While it might appear from this list that *90210* dealt with the complexities of sexual harassment and assault in different forms, the show consistently made one thing perfectly clear: rapists are bad men, and none of the women on the show are friends with bad men. Even the main characters who are accused of rape are ultimately let off the hook and proven to be more or less innocent.

Steve's date rape predicament is presented to viewers as a he said/she said, but it's clear we're supposed to believe Steve. His accuser, Laura, is clingy and pissed that he blew her off after they had sex. The viewer is shown Steve and Laura's points of view as they each narrate a black and white flashback, with the camera focused so close in that we can't quite tell who's doing what. But we know this: the actions in Steve's flashback match what he's saying, while subtle inconsistencies run throughout Laura's.

When Laura is about to reveal Steve as a frat-house rapist at a Take Back the Night march, Kelly cuts her off and tells the crowd how Steve had saved her from the Halloween rapist in high school, and there should be more guys like him. All the radical feminists applaud Steve. In the next scene, Steve apologizes to Laura for leading her on. She says that she thought her life would be so great if she'd just get a frat boy for a boyfriend. Laura admits that while she didn't say yes, she didn't say no, either. But this storyline is not really about shades of gray, about missed signals; it is really about a woman scorned.

In the he said/she said case of Valerie and Noah, it's eventually revealed that Noah's evil brother had roofied Valerie, intending to rape her. (In case the evil brother didn't tip you off, this was one of the show's later asinine plots.) He got called away, and Noah—who was drunk and didn't know Val had been drugged—slept with her. Noah was trashed, they'd slept together before, and he's not the one who drugged her, so the whole thing landed on "I'm sorry this happened to you, but at least I'm not the *real* bad guy."

When David is accused of statutory rape, it's made super clear that the sex was consensual. The girl sneaks into the 21+ club where David DJs, and comes onto him. Like, *hard*, and then goes home with him. It's not until later that he finds out she's seventeen. Dylan goes inappropriately out of his way to defend David, both talking to the girl's parents and tracking her down in school, urging her to admit the truth. Dylan's considered a hero—not a harasser—for doing so, and David is ultimately relieved of all charges.

The "real" rapists, on the other hand, are all bad guys: They are sober, violent, and not particularly handsome. They wield brute strength and ropes and knives. Donna's would-be rapist is lumbering and balding. The football player rapists brandish their popularity as much as their muscles. Kelly's Halloween rapist actually appears as if he *might* be a normal guy who genuinely thought they were role playing for Halloween, and then feels bad and apologizes when he realizes she's not into it. Except after saying all that, he decides to pin Kelly to the bed anyway, making him even more psychotic than we originally thought. Luckily, her friends burst into the room to save her.

In a bevy of mixed messages, Kelly berates herself for dressing sexy and Brenda reminds her that she tried to tell Kelly the dress was "too much" and that she was asking for trouble. Dylan says it doesn't matter how you dress or what you do, a guy always has a choice. Brenda declares that once Kelly said NO, nothing else was her fault—kind of implying it was her fault up until she said no.

The rapist is removed from the party and punched out by Steve. All the other "real" rapists and harassers are fired, killed, or jailed without any lengthy trial the victim must endure. They do not continue hanging out with The Gang, living relatively normal, unaffected lives. And, in the world of *90210*, the same goes for the victims. Within a few episodes, most of the violated women have moved on.

Hate is Just a Four-Letter Word

To say that *90210* had a "spotty" record dealing with race is a massive understatement. Throughout 293 episodes and numerous cast changes, only two cast members of color appeared in the opening credits: one Korean-American woman and one Latino man. Zero Black men or women. On *90210*, Black actors were relegated to minor roles: Willie, the Peach Pit cook and his rapper nephew; Herbert, Steve's freshman buddy who he manipulates into hacking into the school computer; Henry Thomas, the manager of the Beverley Hills Beach Club, who also owns a South Central sporting goods store that burned in the Rodney King riots.

90210 only gave Black people storylines when racial themes needed to be dealt with in Very Special Episode style. One of those Very Special Episodes occurred in season two, when a Black family moves onto the same street as the Walshes. The Ashe family (Get it? Ashe? Not white and not black, but gray?) moved on up from Inglewood because Dad made a shitload of money selling gourmet popcorn. Their younger son, Robbie (played by Eugene Byrd), is a slightly geeky photographer for the *West Beverly Blaze*. The Ashe's oldest, Sherice (played by Vivica A. Fox wearing all sorts of cute hats), still loves her Inglewood boyfriend and doesn't care to assimilate into the family's fancy new zip code. "We moved here so we could become a whiter shade of pale," she sasses to her dad.

"One of the reasons we moved out was to put as many miles as possible between you and that Devo Demars character," her father says sternly. He calls Devo a thug, leaving the viewer to assume he's a crack-dealing, drive-by shooting Crip.

So much about this setup falls apart right away. If Sherice's parents wanted to "put as many miles as possible" between her and Devo, why did they move only ten miles away, instead of, for example, up towards Malibu or down towards Newport? And why did Daddy buy Sherice a shiny new convertible, making it easy to cruise those ten miles down La Cienega to visit Devo at his workplace, Tamale Heaven? And why did they allow Sherice to continue going to school in Inglewood—presumably down the street from Tamale Heaven—instead of transferring to West Beverly High, like her brother? Well, because if they'd done any of that, this Very Special Episode would have no plot.

Brandon meets Sharice when they have a fender bender (she's a careless woman driver with a fiery temper, you know). After some initial tension, he starts flirting with Sherice and asks her out. They stop by the Peach Pit, and The Gang's reaction is kind of appalling—and probably an accurate portrayal of how white kids that age in that era in that zip code would have responded. Kelly half-approvingly/half-bitchily tells Brandon that this is "very hip" of him, and the next day Steve asks if he's got a case of jungle fever. It's uncomfortable to watch, in the way racism should be uncomfortable to watch.

While Sherice is out having a Mega Burger with Brandon, Devo decides to make his way North of Wilshire to visit her. He's never been to her new house and is walking Hillcrest Drive trying to find it, when the private neighborhood security patrol stops him. Devo tells the guards that he has every right to be there, walking with flowers and frozen yogurt for his girlfriend. The security guards get snotty, and Devo throws attitude right back. One of the guards slams him into the hood of his car and growls, "Give me a reason."

Give me a reason to fuck you up, is what he means. Mind you, this was 1991, *waaaay* before George Floyd and Tamir Rice and Trayvon Martin were murdered—but six months after home video was leaked of L.A. police beating the shit out of Rodney King, an unarmed Black man.

I guess Devo gave these asshole security guards "a reason" (he probably, you know, breathed or something) because he ends up in the ER. This part happens off screen, and we only hear about it through a game of telephone tag. Brandon is rightly outraged when the news of

Devo's bogus harassment reaches him, and wants to write a scathing expose for *The West Beverly Blaze*. But he can't get any sources to go on record. Young Robbie doesn't want to talk about it because he feels he's being used and tokenized by Brandon. Sherice won't talk to Brandon because her father told her to sweep the messiness under the rug. "Your mother and I didn't work all these years to buy a house in Beverly Hills so that we would be put under a microscope!" he yells.

All this makes Brandon even more incensed. He keeps telling the Black people that what happened to Devo was *wrong*, and don't they care? Because without this sixteen-year-old white boy, they'd have no idea what discrimination looks like or what their options are in the face of it. Brandon decides to drive to Tamale Heaven and talk to Devo himself. As he pulls his '65 convertible Mustang into the parking lot, three Black boys emerge from the restaurant. Brandon has a weird, supposedly tense stare down with them. We're supposed to believe these kids in their brand-new clothes—one in a coral-pink t-shirt, another with one strap of his denim overalls hanging down exactly the way Dylan did the very first time we met him—and in no way wielding weapons, are menacing. Mostly, I think, they're probably just trying to figure out what the fuck Brandon is doing in Inglewood. Devo comes outside and tells them to step off, as if they were about to unload on Brandon *Pulp Fiction* style.

Devo's kind of awesome. He's a tough guy with muscles, but wears an ear cuff with a dangling peace sign. He even makes fun of Brandon for asking who "jacked him up," returning with, "You've been reading your Spike Lee handbook!" Devo informs Brandon that police harassment is common for him and his friends, and the only thing different about the Rodney King beating was that someone caught it on video. Devo has three brothers: two are in jail, and one is "on the pipe." Devo is his mom's pride and joy, and he doesn't want to make any more waves that would embarrass her (kids standing up against racism is apparently an embarrassment for Black parents).

Brandon ends up getting Robbie's blessing to write the exposé—mostly because he shot a bunch of dope photos to accompany it. Brandon's article convinces Sherice's father to let her date Devo openly because—get this—it helped him "rediscover his roots." It's *soooo* cringy, this idea that it took a white teenager to convince a successful Black man to not be ashamed of where he came from. But this turn of events isn't *supposed* to be uncomfortable, like some of the earlier racist moments. This is supposed to be the happy ending. And the episode does end happily, with The Gang eating gourmet popcorn with Robbie in the Walsh living room, and Jim and Cindy drinking coffee and talking about baseball in the kitchen with Robbie's parents.

Oh, and by the way, we never see Robbie and Sherice or their parents ever again.

Offensive Interference

The other "Brandon is Outraged by Racism!" episode is "Home and Away," in season three. It starts with Brandon delivering a Doogie Howser voiceover, telling us *this was just a weekend like any other weekend.* The West Beverly football team has just won their third game in a row—something they haven't done in eons (actually making it not just like any other weekend, but whatever), and they're pumped to play the fabled and unbeaten Shaw High School in South Central the next weekend. But that night, a shooting occurs at a Shaw game, so the West Beverley board forfeits next weekend's game for the safety of its students.

Brandon is so outraged by the unfairness of the game being cancelled that he drives to South Central to find a compadre at Shaw. Jordan Bonner (played by Michael Anthony Rawlins) is Brandon's newspaper doppelganger, and he's no gang banger; he's smart, not physically imposing, and wears Cross Colours clothes.

When Brandon first shows up, Jordan's like, "You know, Brandon? Brandon of Beverly Hills? You don't know squat." (It's super cute that Jordan says "squat"). They eventually find common ground because super-earnest Brandon has that effect on people. Brandon and Jordan hatch a plan they hope will make a statement and possibly fix this mess that's been going on since 1619. Brandon publicly invites all Shaw students to attend West Bev's Pigskin Prom the night before the cancelled game. *Make a circle*, says Brandon's editorial—like, we'll all join hands and sing Kum Ba Yah and shit.

A bunch of Shaw guys show up at the Pigskin Prom, and everyone acts like a marauding gang just burst through the doors. When a harmless scuffle breaks out, the security guards react with excessive force against the Black kid involved and are told, "No, they're both ours (i.e., West Bev students), let them go!" *Ours*, yikes. (Although, in all fairness, how could they have known Black guys played for West Beverly, since the most seasoned *90210* viewer had never seen them before, either?) But worse than all this racial tension and harassment is that *no one is dancing*. Wait, let me clarify: no one is dancing to David Silver's white boy rap. The dance might just be a total disaster, but it's saved by the girls: Donna, Brenda and Nicky (Brandon's girlfriend du jour) bridge the great divide by asking a couple of the Shaw guys to dance.

This is when it's obvious that very few Black girls came over with the guys from Shaw; only a couple are spotted in the background. Even more, at no point does a white boy ask a Black girl to dance. It's hard for me to work out the reasoning on this one, but somehow *that* was the line the writers/network wouldn't cross?

By the end of "Home and Away," it's a regular ebony and ivory-fest, with everyone doing a weird, coordinated line dance, David rapping with a Shaw kid with actual DJ skills, and the football players deciding to play an unofficial scrimmage at a park the next day.

90210 usually did away with characters of color once they completed their one-episode storyline, but kept Jordan Bonner around after he helped Brandon cure racism. Jordan reappears when Andrea runs into him at a cliché-ridden tea party for Los Angeles students accepted to Yale. They bond over the (unfounded) belief that they're the only two people in the entire room on scholarship. Next thing you know, Andrea and Jordan are dating. And it's very much a "next thing you know" situation. We never see them flirting or courting or kissing.

Jordan conveniently comes down with the flu before he's supposed to take Andrea to prom, making way for Andrea and Brandon to almost hook up (again) and avoiding putting Andrea and Jordan in any romantic situations. *Then* we never see Jordan again.

[Side note: In the 2019 super meta reboot, Gabrielle Carteris says Andrea wasn't even allowed to touch her own Black boyfriend. This is technically untrue; she and Jordan do put their arms around each other and have a couple moments of casual touch. But they never kiss on camera or show the kind of sexual intimacy routinely portrayed between other characters.]

Andrea is a purposeful and perfect co-ed to pair with Jordan. She's smart and liberal and doesn't much care about how things look to other people. But more than that, she's an outsider herself. She's a working-class Jew from the Valley. So, it's okay for her to date someone else who is "other." Which is probably why in season four (The Gang's first year of college), she gets paired off with Mexican-American Jesse Vasquez.

As Andrea's husband and baby daddy, Jesse (Mark Damon Espinoza) was the first character of color to be featured in the opening credits of *90210*. This technically classified him as a "main role," but let's be real: he was always a supporting character to Andrea and her friends. Despite appearing in fifty episodes, Jesse never had his own storylines. He was a law student by day and a bartender at night, but we only saw Jesse in those roles through the eyes of the other characters. If he was lawyering, it's because one of the white kids needed legal help. If he was tending bar, it's because Dylan was trying to get a drink. If he was opining about white privilege and racism, it's because one of The Gang needed to be schooled about how spoiled they are. (Steve. Let's face it, it's almost always Steve.)

During the high school years, *90210*'s only Latinx characters were Ramón, who worked at Tamale Heaven (I swear, I could watch an entire series about Tamale Heaven), the Walsh's maid, Anna, and her niece, Karla. Karla uses the Walsh address to attend West Beverley, and is a romantic interest for Brandon (really, who isn't?). Brandon incorrectly assumes Karla is using the Walsh's address to get a better education than she would in her own district, but it turns out she witnessed a drive-by shooting while volunteering on the East Side and needs to be hidden until she can testify against the bad guy.

When Karla is hired to help Anna cater a party at the Walsh house, Brandon becomes morally incensed, yelling that it's humiliating and condescending. Karla explains to Brandon something along the lines of, "This is my job. It's only humiliating because you have a low view of the help, and what do you know about my life, anyway?" Karla only lasts one episode, and Anna mysteriously disappears after season one.

More characters of color pop up during *90210*'s college years, and the show was even *this close* to having a Black main character. D'Shawn Hardell (Cress Williams) starts out as a cliché—an arrogant and academically lazy basketball player being floated by the permissive faculty because he's a virtuoso on the court. But when he breaks his leg and sees the possibility of his basketball career going up in flames, D'Shawn commits himself to academics—and to not being a dick.

At a society fundraiser in season five, Donna dares to dance with D'Shawn (like, they actually touch each other!). Her uptight mother reprimands her for making a spectacle of herself, reminding Donna that appearances matter. The incident isn't played off as a Very Special Episode—it's not even the primary or secondary plot. Instead, it's used to reveal character, showing Donna individuating from her controlling mother by making her own choices.

Charles Rosin, a writer for the show, said they'd originally planned a romance between D'Shawn and Donna, but it was shot down by Aaron Spelling (Executive Producer, and father to Tori). "He was from Texas, he was from Dallas," Rosin said of Spelling, "He was older, he was courtly, and he you know … was very cautious of some of the stories relating to race that we had." Read between the lines on *that.*

Which brings us to the primary problem with *90210* and many of the issues they tried to tackle: It was a show about Gen X kids, written by late Baby Boomers, and produced by The Greatest Generation. It created a discordance between the stories they wanted to tell, the way they wanted to tell them, and who they were telling them to. At the end of "Ashes to Ashes" Dylan reads aloud a line from Brandon's article: "It's when we stop looking at the human race as individuals that we, as a generation, are in trouble," and the whole gang oohs and aahs about how profound it is.

But Gen Xers wouldn't consider that observation new or profound. This was a generation who grew up watching *All in the Family* and *The Jeffersons* and, yes, Spike Lee movies. It's also unlikely this naïve philosophizing reflected the attitudes of the Boomer writers, who lived through the Freedom Riders and Watts riots and the assassinations of Malcom X and Dr. King.

What it does suggest is that the writers felt Gen X needed to be lectured to. This was the generation that hadn't fought in a war and wasn't disrupting the status quo. We were *slackers.* After Rodney King's beating aired on nighttime news, Gen X didn't take to the streets with signs and bullhorns. Okay, neither did the Boomers, but they'd already paid their dues, and it was up to the next generation to pick up where they left off.

Except we didn't. We watched from our TV screens—something we'd been trained to do since early childhood. We watched a year later when the four officers who'd beaten King were acquitted, and we watched as riots broke out in South Central and the city was looted and burned. For better or worse, we'd been conditioned to learn through *watching*. But we hadn't been taught to act. Acting would have meant abandoning the all-mighty TV. I want to believe Brandon's *Sesame Street*-level lesson was really Boomers imploring Gen X to get off our asses and *do* something, but chances are it was just an easy, feel-good way to wrap up a messier-than-one-episode plot.

The Long Goodbye

90210 was considered the first nighttime teen soap—but it wasn't a soap at first, not really. For its first three years it was a better version of an *Afterschool Special*—a version featuring characters we aspired to be, or be friends with, or who we at least found remotely interesting in a "love to hate" way. The issues were more nuanced than in an *Afterschool Special*, decisions weren't simply good or bad, and the teen sex was, well, *sexier*. But the basic needs were the same: characters struggled to discover their identities amid peers they simultaneously admired, feared, loved, and hated, with parents they simultaneously admired, feared, loved, and hated. Love, sex, drugs, academic pressure, and fitting in were themes we could all relate to, even if they were dressed in the gloss of pretty rich people who had nothing to do with our real lives.

The show lost its way when it abandoned relatable themes. The writers figured they needed to explore "more mature" topics when they sent The Gang off to college. But in real life, the puzzles we try to work out post-high school aren't that much different than the ones we were trying to work out in high school. Whether we were working, attending college, or both, most of us were not, for example, dealing with being sucked into a cult. Or being stalked by a serial rapist. Or being blackmailed by a professor who thinks we're sleeping with his wife (who we do end up sleeping with). Most of us don't own a nightclub while attending school full time, or in the course of one year lose our virginity, become pregnant, get married, have a dangerously premature baby, have an affair, reconcile with our husband, and move away. We don't get trapped in house fires, we don't get held hostage by our crazy rehab roommate, and we don't extort ex-lovers for $100,000. We *really* don't end up in a sword fight in Mexico with a con man who embezzled our millions of dollars, nor do we watch our wife be accidentally murdered by thugs her father hired to kill us.

This, the college years, is when *90210* made the turn towards becoming a true soap opera. Sure, sometimes amid the "this shit doesn't actually happen to anyone" theatrics, they still threw in real-life scenarios: Being in love with the wrong person. Tanking in school. Learning about animal rights and human rights. Asserting our independence. Being afraid of what comes next. Facing adulthood. But it's telling that by the fifth episode of season nine, the show didn't feature a single member of the family it was founded on: Jim and Cindy Walsh were living in Hong Kong, Brenda was in London, and Brandon in Washington, D.C. The realest people in Beverly Hills no longer lived in Beverly Hills.

In the nineties, no producer set out to make a series with a limited run. More often than not, shows ended because their ratings plummeted or they'd been on so long even the actors and writers could no longer muster interest. Jason Priestley said one of the reasons he left *90210* early in season nine was because he "didn't want the show to become an over-the-top nighttime drama where Steve Sanders is in a coma, and all of a sudden his twin brother shows up." But by that time, Priestley had already executive produced the episodes where Kelly gets selective amnesia after being shot, unable to remember that Brandon is the love of her life. Priestley got out of that sticky mess too late.

It's easy to for me to say two decades later that what they really *should* have done was continue *90210* as a show about high schoolers. If they hadn't been so insistent on making The Gang graduate at the same time, they could have easily followed some to college, while others were still back at West Beverly. They could have ended *Beverly Hills, 90210* before it had worn out its welcome, letting the show drive off into a Pacific sunset still young and pretty and desired.

Part III

*You have sung to me in my aloneness,
and I of your longings have built a tower
in the sky.*

—Kahlil Gibran

Blood Brothers

The Denver Post, The New York Times, Newsweek, Vanity Fair—these are some of the results that popped up when I Googled my high school friend, Rachel. It was 2001, and Googling people was still new, thrillingly subversive, and kind of creepy. I hadn't seen Rachel since we graduated in 1985. *I wonder what she's up to?* I thought. *What ever happened to Rachel?*

The Google results featured headlines with words like *sorrow* and *killer* and *hate*. The reason for these weighted words was Rachel's youngest brother, Elias. In all those articles, Rachel was asked about her skinhead brother who had shot a cop and committed suicide amid a hail of gunfire in 1997.

It seemed like I'd stumbled across a secret—a shame whispered but never spoken. It was the exact reason that Googling people is creepy, because we become two-dimensional voyeurs into the root of others' most complex pain. It turned out Rachel and I were living just 110 miles away from each other in Oregon, so I sent her a note saying something like, "We're so close by, would love to see you!" I drove down I-5 to her house, and we spent several hours madly catching up while eating sun-warmed grape tomatoes plucked from her yard.

Rachel taught at a Waldorf school and lived with her boyfriend, a potter. Her dad had died in 1991 and her mother still lived in Denver; my mom had died in 1994 and my dad still lived in Denver. Her other brother, Max, lived in a former railroad town in the Rockies; my older brother lived with our dad. I didn't ask Rachel about Elias. Surely it was too sensitive, the grief too blinding. It had been less than five years since he'd died, and the chronology of grief runs the opposite of geologic time: so much slower than everyone else's lived experience. Five years of grief is a cosmic blip.

At least another year passed before I finally asked Rachel about Elias. It was when she came to stay with me and my husband in Portland for a night. She sat on our shabby chic purple couch, her blond hair curly and thick, her blues eyes bright. She and Elias had looked alike, except for more than a foot difference in their height. And, maybe, Elias lacked that same brightness in his eyes.

I broached the topic so seriously, so carefully: "I came across these articles about your brother." I don't remember Rachel's exact words, so much as her tone: not forbidding, but not impassioned either. *Yes, it's okay to talk about this. No, I am not still traumatized.*

My mother had died eight years earlier, and I was still stricken. I didn't know that by 2011 my dad and brother would die, too, marking the end of my family. But maybe there was some wormhole in the chronology of grief that let me glimpse my impending losses. Maybe that's why I became obsessed with understanding how Elias died and Rachel survived.

✝

Rachel's brother was twenty-five when he died, mine was forty-five. Elias abused the kinds of drugs that hype you up—meth and coke— while Steve abused the kinds that bring you down—barbiturates, booze, opioids. Elias died from a bullet that entered beneath his chin and barreled to his brain. Steve died from two emboli that started in his thigh and migrated to his lungs. Elias died in the middle of the afternoon, crouched in an alcove at a condominium complex, surrounded by one hundred law enforcement officers. My brother died in the middle of the night in the house we grew up in, alone in his bed.

They died one thousand feet from each other.

When I first discovered all the articles about Elias, my obsessive focus was, "What is it like to lose your brother in such a horrific way?" I didn't know I was going to lose my brother sooner than later, and while the manner wouldn't in any way resemble a scene from a steroidal action movie, it would be achingly sad. Most of the articles I read about Elias weren't really about how the survivors survive. The articles published in the immediate aftermath focused on: Skinhead Leads Cops on High-Speed Chase and Kills Veteran Police Officer. The next round of articles—spanning from a month after the bedlam to two years later—pondered the question: What happened to make this young man from a liberal, peace-loving family become a white supremacist?

It took me a good fifteen years to arrive at the same question. Or, at least, for that question to push aside the question of how we survive loss. It was the fall of 2017, and a racism that had apparently been lurking in the shadows was now walking in bright daylight. People of color weren't as surprised as white liberals. They were like, "Yeah, we *know* people are unrelentingly racist, you dumb-dumbs." White liberals were more whiplashed. We assumed that kind of racism only existed in a small number of underground niches that could be contained, like an annoying game of Whack-a-Mole where the prize for winning was a false sense of security.

Because I am the sort of person who is always looking for causes, humanity, rapprochements, I thought that if I could understand how Elias became a white supremacist, then I could understand how we, the U.S., got here. What I failed to recognize in this impulse is that with Elias, there was no great rapprochement. There was only his twenty-five-year-old body in a stairwell, and a police officer pronounced DOA.

But it was nonetheless the motivation I told myself when I emailed Rachel in 2017 and asked if I could interview her about Elias. I wanted to investigate a problem less myopic than grief.

✛

Rachel and I knew each other throughout high school, mostly through shared classes and friends. I was only in her house once. It was senior year and I'd driven her home late at night. I'm not sure why I went inside—maybe I was stoned and needed water to quench my dry mouth. Rachel's family house was written about a lot after Elias died— being called everything from a "Neo-Georgian Mansion" to a "witch house of Satan"—so I've thought about it more than you'd usually think about a house you'd only been in for a few minutes. My dusty memories are of a two-story red brick exterior and white portico that belonged in colonial Williamsburg more than Denver. A long path led us to the front door, to arched doorways, old wood furniture, and rooms divided by French doors. The house was quiet and dark, Rachel's parents asleep upstairs. I don't know where her younger brothers were. I didn't know it at the time, but Max, the one closest in age to Rachel, was already involved with the Denver Skins. Soon her youngest brother, Elias, would be, too. But perhaps, right then, Elias was tucked away in bed, safe.

After high school, I went to college in Oregon, and Rachel stayed in Denver. The distance between us was 981 miles as the crow flies. We are not crows, however; we are bound to the ground.

✛

When I emailed Rachel twenty years after Elias died and asked if I could interview her, she said she'd talk to me, but wanted me to use pseudonyms for her and her family members. It was not just her story, she said. Her family had been traumatized, and she didn't want them randomly running across my essay and being re-traumatized.

I tell you this so you know: names have been changed not to protect the innocent or the guilty, but to protect the broken hearts and bruised souls of those left behind.

✛

Rachel's mother, who is consistently described as a kind and deeply caring person, was a Waldorf School teacher, and Rachel's father was a well-loved pastor at a church. The philosophy behind both their institutions was freedom of thought and responsibility to the community. They were inclusive and peace loving, open to people of all genders and races. This is how Rachel and her bothers were raised.

One of the peculiarities about the Waldorf model is that it teaches children to read when each individual child seems developmentally ready. The whole curriculum strives to meet the respective child wherever they are in their process, and Elias's process was always way behind the curve. He told Rachel that he didn't really learn to read until he was eighteen, in jail. In an interview, their mother said Elias had suffered from dyslexia, although as a child he never received an official diagnosis—which means he received no intervention or treatment.

"Stephen reads well, but his related independent work was often done carelessly and with poor penmanship and spelling," teachers wrote on my brother's elementary school report cards. "Pupil is achieving below apparent ability," and "he loses temper, cries when corrected. Definitely needs to work on self control." Under "Parent Comments," my mom wrote: *Steve's difficulties with self control is something we are aware of and we work with him at home to try to help him improve.*

Our parents sent Steve to the Evans Learning Center. I was also evaluated, although at the time I didn't know why. My grades were solid, and at that age I didn't have any serious social problems. My hearing was tested and I moved colored pegs around a board and a therapist watched me play with dolls to see what kind of scenarios I created. Now that I have examined the deep crevasses of my family dynamics, I suspect the reason I was also tested is because my parents didn't want Steve to feel singled out, weird.

I never returned after my initial assessment, but Steve went once a week for a while. He was diagnosed as "hyper" (which, back in those days, was short for "hyperactive child" or "hyperkinetic child"), and my parents had to watch his intake of substances that might have a stimulating effect, like Pepsi or cough medicine with alcohol. Now I realize Steve was diagnosed with what we presently call Attention Deficit Hyperactivity Disorder (ADHD), and I suspect what the therapists were really seeing in him were the nascent signs of bipolar disorder—poor attention, racing thoughts, fidgeting, increase in irritability, a need for grandiosity.

"Eli's learning disorder seems really important to me," Rachel said. "Because I feel if that had been addressed better, he might have had more guidance moving through the more socially acceptable channels of life. But because it wasn't addressed at all, he *really* struggled in school, and I think it wasn't very long before he figured out that the underground world was going to be an easier way to make his path."

My brother wasn't drawn to the underground world. He yearned to fit into mainstream society—Polo shirts and a blue Jeep Cherokee and Paula Abdul and golf. But his brain and his body were too chaotic, and his easiest path was forged by booze. Gambling. Working for and living with our dad. Buying drinks for everyone at the bar, so by the end his only friends were other barely-employed alcoholics.

Elias's struggles also weren't just academic. As a child, he was never violent, nor did he have emotional outbursts, but sometimes he would sit motionless for a long time, staring at someone without saying a word. The behavior followed him into adulthood. Sometimes Rachel would have to sit next to him for an hour or longer before he'd speak to her.

"Do you think he was on the spectrum?" I asked.

"I've never thought of that before," she said. "But it makes total sense."

It's interesting the things we see from outside, and are clouded to from within. I'm sure Rachel has thought about her brother—what went wrong, why he was the way he was, how the tragedy could have been prevented—a thousand times. She's an educator working with young children, herself. These days, being "on the spectrum" is the first conclusion we jump to for every emotional and cognitive difference. And if not that, then the plethora of other diagnoses—Executive Functioning Disorder, Dysgraphia, Social Communication Disorder, etc.—none of which Rachel had previously applied to Elias.

From the twenty-first century it seems strange that Rachel's mother, also an educator, didn't see the need for any testing or intervention for young Eli's problems. She embraced the paradigm that there wasn't something *wrong* with him that needed fixing. He was just different, and differences in children should be nurtured, not squashed or shamed. Which sounds sort of *lovely*—until it's not.

✛

Denver didn't have a Waldorf high school in the eighties, so when Rachel finished eighth grade, she had to forsake that intimate, creative environment. Moving to a massive public high school seemed dizzying and destabilizing, so she instead applied for a scholarship at the small prep school where we ultimately met. She said she barely passed the entrance exam, which seems impossible. Rachel was so smart. She willingly took *Latin*, for god's sake. But Waldorf didn't use standardized learning or testing, so our school's entrance exam proved a formidable hurdle.

When it came time for her oldest brother, Max, to commence to high school, he failed our school admissions test twice. The public school he'd be funneled into, Denver's South High, was big and impersonal and not exactly known for its excellence in academics. So, their parents sent him to live with a family in New York City and attend a Waldorf school there.

This is such a critical junction in the story of Elias, the part where I stop and wonder: *What if?*

The family Max lived with in New York didn't really want a teenager or know how to interact with one. He felt unwelcome, not a part of a family system. He also suspected he'd been sent away because his parents didn't want him around. *We are both so busy with our work, we simply don't have time to usher this boy into manhood. Let him be someone else's problem.* Max ran away from the New York family's house and lived in Central Park for a week or so, adrift, unwanted, angry, and so, so, so vulnerable.

He met a group of other young men living in the park who welcomed him into their ranks. Their offer was one of friendship, of protection, of inclusion. They created their own power, and would stick up for each other no matter what. They were a brotherhood.

When Max returned to Denver, he quickly found that same kind of brotherhood with the Denver Skins—much to his older sister's astonishment. Rachel had heated discussions with him around the dining room table, where he'd expound on his racist views. "I'd be just shocked," she said, "and horrified and so opposed."

Sometimes Elias would be at the table with them, and sometimes he'd be in his room. When he was at the table, Elias would sit quietly, rarely speaking. Every once in a while, he might say something that made Rachel think he agreed with Max, but she really wasn't sure. "I never really took the time, I guess, to find out his full story."

What struck me about this scene is that their parents weren't in it. It's not like the kids were being raised by single or divorced parents. There was no practical reason for them to be latchkey. But there they were at dinner time, with Elias in his room and Rachel and Max arguing about his extreme racism, and their parents detached from it all.

Rachel manages to strike a balance in recognizing her parents' shortcomings—and their lack of intervention—without resorting to words like "guilt" or "blame." As a matter of fact, she said that phrase—*I don't blame them*—often. "It was just enough parenting for someone who was doing okay … but for my brothers, who struggled, it really wasn't enough."

When Elias finished eighth grade, there wasn't a moment's thought that he could get into an academically challenging school. Max's NYC debacle proved that sending Elias away was also a bad idea, so off to South High School he went. He was placed in remedial classes, where his classmates were overwhelmingly Black and Hispanic. Elias was teased and bullied and ended up dropping out in tenth grade. Then he looked to his older brother, Max, who had all these friends rooted in power and brotherhood, and didn't that sound like a better option?

The critical juncture: *What if?* What if Max had not been sent to New York and found the boys in the park and come back to Denver wanting more of what he found? Who would Elias have slid in with, then? And what I really mean by these questions: Would Elias—and the police officer he shot—still be alive?

✛

What would it have taken for my brother to still be alive? In one scenario, I trace it back to when he was first diagnosed with bipolar disorder, at age forty, and was prescribed lithium. My dad didn't like how it made Steve slower, more lethargic, in those first couple of weeks, so he convinced him to stop taking it. "Whatever this thing is, we'll beat it on willpower alone," my dad said. Maybe if Steve had stayed on the lithium, then he wouldn't have been tortured by paranoia that the hip replacement surgeries he desperately needed would kill him. He wouldn't have been in and out of the hospital so many times that his body became a breeding ground for life-threatening infections. Steve might not have become addicted to opioids, and might not have lain in bed for two years straight, inviting those two pulmonary emboli to race to his lungs.

But maybe that wasn't the critical juncture with Steve. Maybe it was when he was fifteen and started drinking and quit football and distanced himself from his friends. Maybe if he'd gotten psychiatric intervention then, he could have lived a relatively normal life. He could have had a career and a wife and kids. But the thing is, when Steve was fifteen my dad was still who he was, too. His identity was tied too closely to his son, the stigma of mental illness too shameful. It was better to just pretend everything was okay.

✦

There's almost a *and the next thing you know* twist to Rachel's family story. Like, "and the next thing you know, both her brothers were dealing drugs and arms."

What?

I've known a fair amount of drug dealers in my days—pot, coke, pills, acid—but to the best of my knowledge have never known an arms dealer. I've always thought of arms dealers as international cartels and shadowy governments providing millions of dollars of military grade weapons to insurgents in the middle east. But just like there are Pablo Escobar-level coke dealers *and* there's the guy moving a recreational gram here and there, there are also petty arms dealers. The Denver Skins were a cog in that gun-peddling machinery.

It's not clear how much Rachel's parents knew about their sons' cache of guns hidden in their own house. In their hands-off parenting style, they weren't the type to go snooping in their kids' rooms—especially by the time the kids were adults. "I believe my parents had a lot of trust that everything would turn out all right," Rachel said. "And in this situation, it needed a lot more than trust."

Rachel *did* know about the guns, something she now feels a lot of responsibility about. "I didn't want to tell on them. But I feel now the best thing would have been to tell anyone who would listen, to prevent disaster."

It seems blatantly obvious in hindsight, from the outside, but maybe not so much in 1997. This was before Columbine High School and the Century 16 movie theater and Walmart and the Gilroy Garlic Festival had become shooting galleries for angry young men.

✛

Max eventually lessened his involvement with the Denver Skins. He went back to school and enrolled in some college classes. Rachel said it opened up his mind and "created a whole other conversation for him." He got married and became a father, and ran a company that hired out roadies for rock bands.

Elias still ran with the Skins and dealt drugs and guns and got arrested plenty of times. He also started hanging out with the Suns of Darkness, an all-Black motorcycle club. The Suns weren't a violent criminal gang, like the Mongols or Hell's Angels. Their stated priorities were: "Family, job, religion, Suns of Darkness." But being Black and organized is not something law enforcement looks upon kindly. Suns were constantly pulled over and harassed for minor infractions, which didn't make them look too kindly on cops, in return.

Elias adopted an older member of the Suns as his surrogate father, a man who attended his funeral. How in the world could Elias be a skinhead—with a swastika tattooed on his chest—and simultaneously choose this Black man as his de-facto dad? Rachel doesn't know. My best guess for this blaringly bizarre contradiction is that Elias adopted the ideology of whoever would accept him, and the Suns accepted him because he was a kindred spirit on the margins of society. When Elias was being nurtured in the Waldorf School, he welcomed peace and openness.

When the Skins embraced him as a teen and young adult, he embraced their racism. And once Elias found a place among the Suns of Darkness, he shifted to their point of view: the cops are out to get you.

✥

If you're white, and you're smart, and you're lucky, you can sell drugs and guns for a pretty long time before getting caught. Elias was only the first of that trifecta. He was arrested several times for possession of a concealed weapon, dealing drugs and guns, third-degree assault, criminal mischief, and felony menacing. The media reported that he'd served up to one hundred days in jail by the time he was twenty-five, but Rachel couldn't verify that. She'd only read that number in the papers, just like everyone else. One of Elias's arrests became legendary in the media, a story that was told time and time again.

In the summer of 1993, Elias threw a party at his parents' house when they were out of town. The fireworks and music prompted a neighbor to call the police. When the two responding officers stepped out of their car, they heard someone say, "Sic 'em!" and the family dog raced toward them. Elias was the only person they saw nearby, so they arrested him.

When I mentioned this story, Rachel said, "Oh, that was so weird! Suddenly no one knew where Eli was. He didn't even call us."

"Wait, you were there?" I asked.

"I was there." They'd all assumed Eli had just fallen asleep under a bush. Whenever he got overwhelmed, he'd go find a quiet place to curl up.

The media consistently called this "a skinhead party," so I asked Rachel if it was. "There were some friends of my brothers there who considered themselves Skins," she said. But there were also several of their peace-loving Waldorf classmates from childhood. And there was Rachel. That's when it occurred to me that the officers never went inside the party. They saw Elias outside, they arrested him, they left. So why did every media outlet refer to it as a skinhead party?

One article reported that Elias told the officers during the ride to jail that they'd just stumbled on a skinhead party back there. "Like the KKK?" they asked. Elias said the KKK was too mild for him and his friends. His crew was into more violent stuff. I don't doubt that Elias was stupid enough to say all this to two cops. He was a young man filled with anger and alienation and bravado. But what I doubt is the absolute certainty with which the details of this conversation were repeated by numerous news outlets. Because by the time the story was being told, only one of the three people in that car was still alive. That's why this skinhead party story is often told.

✛

What are the stories that get told about my brother again and again? How he'd drive downtown with all the car windows down singing "Danka Schoen" into the twenty-degree night. Arriving in South Bend Indiana for a Notre Dame game and immediately picking up the motel phone to call some dude named Fast Eddie. How he hovered in the background when a nineteen-year-old guy hit on his fourteen-year-old sister, who'd lied about her age. How he asked for extra gravy at Popeye's and the manager told him, with utter sincerity, "The gravy is *extremely* expensive, sir," and because we laughed the first time he told it, Steve told it again and again.

There are other stories, ones with less joy. Ones where he kicked me out of our family house hours after our mom died and told me never to come back. When he threatened to beat up our dad at 3 a.m. because he'd dared to admonish Steve for driving drunk. When his legs swelled to the size of tree trunks and his skin blistered with giant ulcers. When he was hospitalized for an OD and I asked to speak to the doctor on call, and Steve told me I was always interfering in his life and to leave him alone. And there was the story the coroner told in his autopsy report: "The body is that of a well-developed, obese, Caucasian male who weighs 402 pounds, is 72 inches in length, and appears compatible with the stated age of 45 years. Found lying supine in his bedroom at 0330 hours on August 29, 2011. The body is received unclad. A gray shirt has been cut away and is found underneath the body. The body is cool to the touch. Rigor is fully fixed in all extremities and jaw. The scalp hair is brown and measures 1 inch in length over the crown. The decedent was pronounced dead at the scene."

✣

Here's the story of how Elias ended up dead in an alcove: His friend Bob asked if he'd help Gretchen, a woman he knew, move away from her abusive boyfriend. Elias didn't know Gretchen before that day. Gretchen and the abusive boyfriend both lived in the mountains in a dilapidated lodge with an assortment of other misfits doing forestry work. Bob and another guy drove up to the mountains in a black Chevy, and Elias drove Gretchen in a red Trans Am that the media would refer to as "stolen"—although when and where and who he stole it from was never disclosed.

That day, Elias's 200-pound, 76-inch body was clad in a long-sleeved red shirt, black jeans, a black jacket, a black leather belt, and black boots. He wore two rings—maybe three—on his right hand. It was hard to tell from the crime scene pictures I found. Those pictures of his bloody body in the blood-stained stairwell are the only reason I know what Elias was wearing on the day he died.

He stood by the red Trans Am smoking a cigarette outside the lodge while the others helped Gretchen retrieve her belongings. They apparently broke into the abusive boyfriend's room. It might have been to get back items Gretchen had left in there, the way people involved in intimate relationships leave stuff at each other's places. It might have been specifically to steal shit. The stealing might have been the guys' idea, or it might have been Gretchen's. Either way, they took a major pair of bolt cutters to a major lock on his room, and stole two Yamaha stereo speakers, a guitar amp, three camcorders, and a snowboard.

Elias and Gretchen started back down the mountain in the Trans Am just as a neighbor called in a burglary at the lodge. A sheriff's car started following them. What happened next was influenced by three salient factors: 1) Elias's already long list of arrests; 2) The potent mixture of coke, pot, and meth in his bloodstream; 3) The three guns he'd stashed in the car, including a Chinese SKS semi-automatic rifle underneath his seat.

The SKS is a carbine with a twenty-inch barrel and a self-loading bolt that feeds a ten-round clip. Elias had modified his SKS with a thirty-round clip. When the sheriff started pursuing him, Elias sped up to 100 mph, pulled out the SKS, and told Gretchen to take the wheel. He squeezed off a few shots and the sheriff faded back. But it's not like the sheriff just said, "Oh well, I guess I'll give up on that guy driving bat-out-of-hell and shooting at me." No—he radioed the whole scenario in to the Denver Police Department. In the meantime, Elias sped through Denver, hit cars, backed up, sped off again, and ultimately pulled into a condominium complex one thousand feet from my dad and brother's house.

Immediately to the north of where Elias stopped the car—and, I mean, a matter of *feet* away—was the field where my brother played Pee Wee football. My parents would sit on the sidelines in mesh and aluminum fold-out chairs we'd carried from our house, and I'd play cheerleader to the boys. Five hundred feet south of where Elias parked was the Baskin-Robbins my family rode our bikes to in the summer. My favorite flavor was chocolate, and my mom's was burgundy cherry; my brother liked maple walnut and my dad often got vanilla. One thousand feet southwest of where Elias parked the red Trans Am was the burger joint where I had my first job, busing tables and taking orders for cheeseburgers and onion rings and shakes. These are all ridiculously idyllic middle-class images, the best of my family by a longshot, contrasted with the worst of Rachel's.

A *Vanity Fair* article claims Elias would have gotten away with all this mayhem were it not for two officers arresting prostitutes over on East Colfax who heard the Sheriff's call and busted over in Elias's direction. That seems ridiculous, especially if you know the layout of Denver. East Colfax is eight miles north of where Elias came blazing into town, and I bet there were other cops closer than the two on East Colfax—other cops who heard a guy was *shooting at a sheriff* with a semi-automatic weapon—and thought it was worth checking out. Weirdly, a true crime documentary based on the *Vanity Fair* article claims a police officer cruising in the same neighborhood of the condo heard the radio call, saw the Trans Am pull into the parking lot, and realized what he'd stumbled onto. But why the *Vanity Fair* article and the film about the *Vanity Fair* article aren't on the same page is only a microcosm of the mystery of that afternoon. Of Elias.

Elias probably drove to the condominium complex because it's where his friend Bob lived and where they'd started the day. It's nonetheless a curiously doomed decision, because once Elias pulled into that complex, he was cornered inside a maze. Elias and Gretchen ran towards Bob's door, and the next round of cops to show up yelled at them to come out with their hands up. Gretchen did, and a cop wrestled her into the snow. She wasn't resisting, but the whole adrenaline ejaculation of this situation was just getting started. She was cuffed and thrown in the back of a squad car. Elias ran into an alcove near apartment A, and one hundred police officers descended on, and around, him.

One hundred.

Over the years I've tried to imagine the pandemonium, the men in black riot gear, the sirens, the guns drawn, the helicopters overhead, the K-9 officers running across snowy grass, the streets blocked off, the children at the elementary school next door—were they in lockdown? Did schools even *have* a lockdown drill back then?—the other residents of the complex, some watching *Oprah* or trying to nap or do their laundry. And I imagine my dad and brother, just down the street.

A few years later, Rachel went and stood in the alcove by apartment A. Eli was so trapped, she said—literally cornered, his back to the wall. He only had two choices: He could put down his SKS and come out with his hands behind his head, get wrestled into the snow, kneed in the back, face shoved into the ground, cuffed, thrown in a car, and then thrown in jail—again. Or he could shoot.

Elias shot and he shot and he shot, and the one hundred police officers shot back.

At one point in this frenetic gun battle, a police officer crept around the corner towards Elias. Because I promised Rachel I would use pseudonyms, I will use one for this officer, too. I admit it seems unfair. I admit he deserves to be remembered. In this story his name is Officer James Aldert. Coincidentally, James Aldert was one of the cops who had arrested Elias five years earlier, outside the "skinhead party" at his parents' house.

Elias fired at James Aldert, and hit the upper right side of his head.

A fellow officer said Aldert didn't even fall over immediately. It was more like his body crumpled slowly to the ground. In James Aldert's autopsy, it was revealed that he was shot both from the front (Elias's direction), and from the back (his colleagues'), and that the bullets in his body came from different guns. But no matter those other bullets, Elias had shot a cop and that cop was dead.

Everything that happened after that was, and still is, confusing to me. Every time I read one account it makes sense, until I walk away and remember another report. It's been written that during the gun battle, one Denver police officer went in and retrieved James Aldert's body. It was also reported that two SWAT officers dragged him out. It's been written that the gun battle went on for some time. It's been written that there were three hours of silent standoff before law enforcement found Elias's body dead of a self-inflicted gunshot, his black jacket crumpled at his feet. The official report said Elias had taken Officer Aldert's revolver and killed himself.

How was it that James Aldert's body was riddled with ten bullet wounds from different directions and different guns, but the only gunshot Elias suffered was the one he delivered to himself? If he'd stolen Officer Aldert's revolver, then it would have been after James was killed, but before his body was pulled out. How was Elias not shot when he went for that gun? How did the other officer—or SWAT team—not get shot while retrieving their fallen colleague's body? Did they manage to coordinate a cease fire? Isn't it strange that they were able to get that close to where Elias was huddled with his gun—from where he shot James Aldert—and not get shot, too? Why did it take three hours of *nothing happening* for the police to realize Elias was also dead? And when did Elias have time to take off his jacket?

What I often wonder is what my dad and brother were doing during this three-plus hour standoff. The event was on the news—and my dad watched the news all the time—and surely the helicopters flying overhead made them all the more aware that something *serious* was going down nearby. Another question I often ponder: Did my dad and brother know Elias was dead before Rachel did? But I can't ask them, because by the time I started asking questions, they were gone, too.

✝

"The interesting dichotomy of Eli's whole life story is that so much of the time he was sedentary and outwardly peaceful," Rachel said. Mellow in a stoned way, and so sedentary that he'd sleep until noon, eat a gigantic meal, and then go back to bed, only emerging again before dark if his dad made him mow the lawn, or some other domestic chore. "And then I'd hear through Max that he'd have these outbursts of violence."

"Do you think he was bipolar?" I asked. This is my way: Find the hole that wasn't plugged. What leak did the hole lead to? What happens when that leak becomes a flood?

"I don't think so," Rachel said, "because he didn't have manic phases." Just depressive ones.

"But what about the violence?" My own brother calling our dad at 3 a.m. from a payphone somewhere downtown because he'd gotten in a fight, lost his wallet, lost his keys.

"Oh, maybe," Rachel said. She was quiet, with the thoughtful stillness I'd come to recognize as her thinking deeply, of replaying tapes, of looking for the story within them. "Yes."

Mentally ill people are not inherently violent, nor are people with neurodevelopmental disorders. Studies prove this time-and-time again. But when someone is suffering the effects of mental illness or a cognitive disorder and it isn't recognized, it isn't *treated*, they might go looking for something that will help quell the anxiety and insecurity and depression and mania, something that will calm the chaos in their heads. My brother found money and alcohol, Elias found brotherhood and meth. And *those* things can, and do, lead to violence.

It's theorized that males don't reach full brain development until they're twenty-six years old—an age Elias never reached. Rachel suspects that if he'd lived, he might have grown out of some of the more extreme ways of thinking and being, like Max. Elias had often talked about wanting to live in the woods, maybe in the northwest, and being self-sufficient. "I think he would have loved that lifestyle," Rachel said, "hunting and fishing and living simply in some cabin." But Elias wasn't the kind of person who made things happen for himself. Not until that day in the Trans Am, in the alcove.

Max suffered from deep depression for nearly ten years after Elias died. He finally found an outlet for his anger and depression by talking with a street preacher set up in a dilapidated coffee shop. The preacher even suggested that Max would be a good minister—like his father—for the tattooed and pierced punks, ravers, skaters, and homeless youth. But Max didn't want to proselytize. Rachel didn't fall to depression or anger, but coped through avoidance. It was easier to smoke pot and tune out, she said. Her husband felt she'd never fully dealt with Elias's demise.

"What would that look like?" I asked. "Fully dealing with it?"

"He wishes I would ask my mom more hard questions," Rachel said. He wished Rachel would talk to her mom about their regrets, maybe even broach the unspoken word: guilt. But that's not how their family operated. Both her parents were conflict-avoidant. It's why they didn't intervene in the violent aspects of their son's lives.

There was a time when Max was convinced Eli hadn't killed himself, but that he was shot by police fire. He watched tapes, read transcripts, became obsessed with the idea of a cover-up. "I don't know if it ultimately matters," Rachel said. "My family agrees Eli was living with a death wish that day, by the way he conducted himself . . . because how else could it have ended? So, I don't know if it matters who pulled the trigger."

What matters is that day a decorated police officer died, and Elias died, and Gretchen was imprisoned for her role in the events. All that was left was assigning or withholding blame, shouldering guilt, and entombing pain. I know this, because even with all the mistakes my dad made, all the times he failed to constructively intervene in Steve's life or did so in destructive ways, I don't—I can't stand to—blame him for my brother's death. Rachel and her family have to live with the truth that Elias killed a man. In a tiny recess of my brain that I keep locked for the sake of my sanity, I know that my dad contributed to Steve's death. But, more often than not, I choose to think of my brother's demise as a mysterious combination of nature and nurture, of what did and didn't happen, of what could have been.

Flights of Two

From across the Willamette River at night, Oaks Amusement Park shines with the garish brilliance of the iconic *Great Gatsby* cover. The glimmer of the antique Ferris wheel and the ominous glow of carnival games pulse like dying stars from light-years away. That's the night-tide tableau from across the river, from Portland's west side. But on this day, I was inside the grounds on a June afternoon, and the east side amusement park was closed.

Leaves blew past empty midway booths where, that night, children would fail to win a goldfish or a mood ring or a cheaply-made stuffed bear, and maybe they would cry and maybe they wouldn't care at all. The grotesque carousel horses appeared as if some demonic force had frozen them mid-air, rendering them powerless to gallop away. The spider ride was suspended in a state of rigor mortis, reminding me of an accident in a Denver amusement park when I was six. A leg of the spinning spider had broken off, sending two adults and three children crashing to the ground. On this afternoon, nothing twirled, nothing twinkled, nothing glittered. The dormancy gave it—me—the feeling of existing outside time and space.

The only place open in all of Oaks Park was the oldest roller rink in the country, which was hosting the last day of competition for the Northwest Regional Championships for Artistic Roller Skating. We're not talking women's roller derby, a once working-class sport now co-opted by urban hipsters, or roller blading in any of its recreational or extreme manifestations. This was artistic skating, dance skating, figure skating, on four wheels. Quads, they're called. I came to watch Robert Sitton compete; I came because of yoga and death and loss and love.

Robert and I had been in the same yoga class for nine months. In my mid-forties, I was one of the youngest students twisting and contorting on the sticky mats. I guess most people my age either didn't have the time, or didn't have enough tension in their bodies, to spend a weekday morning attempting to untwist all that has gotten twisted. I'd only been in the class a few weeks when it came up that Robert—gray-haired with adult children—was a competitive dance roller skater. I'd never heard of such a thing. I didn't ask for details because I didn't want to interact with anyone. My dad had been dead for three months and my mom had been gone for fourteen years; my brother was suffering from severe mental and physical illness, predicting his imminent demise. The most I could do was rest in child's pose with my forehead on the floor and let the idle chatter float past my ears.

But nine months later it was spring and my brother was, for the moment, still alive and I wanted to take things in—odd things, unknown things, living things. When Robert mentioned roller skating again, I said, "Wow, how'd you get into *that*?"

"My brother took me skating when I was a kid," Robert said, elongating his already long limbs on a purple mat. "On the sidewalks. I skated whenever I could."

My first sidewalk skates were rickety metal devices that lashed to my Keds with a thin leather strap. The aluminum wheels were so soft they became dented by the pebbles I rolled over on suburban concrete.

Robert bent one knee, twisted his spine. "When I got older, I was looking for a hobby and I figured it needed to be a form of exercise, and I figured it should also be something I love."

Love—that word stuck with me. The *way* he said it stuck with me, as if the asana/prana/pranayama air lifted it toward the skylight pouring sunshine into the studio. Was it really possible for a senior citizen—for anyone other than a child—to *love* roller skating? Since the onset of my family's demise, I hadn't felt love or passion for much, especially anything reminiscent of innocence and youth. Childhood was too precious a place to visit, the realities of adulthood too divergent, that space in between too sad.

Another classmate piped in that her housekeeper competed in dance skating. "Her name is Angie."

"Angie Officer," Robert said, without the slightest acknowledgment that this sounds like a classic porn name. "Oh, sure. I know her."

That meant there were *other* people involved. What did I think? That Robert was out there on the roller rink by himself, competing against himself, perhaps being judged by himself? No. The participants were walking among everyday folks. Taking yoga and cleaning our houses.

"I'd like to see you skate sometime," I said.

"There's this event coming up at Oaks Park," Robert said. "You should come."

✛

The oldest roller rink in the country was dimly lit, and the bleachers metal, backless, torture devices that rendered it impossible to either sit up or slouch comfortably. Tinny recorded organ music leaked out of grainy loudspeakers, even though an impressive 1955 Wurlitzer organ with four keyboards and 1,242 pipes on a platform was suspended precariously over the center of the rink. The entire place smelled like Fritos. It was the fourth and final day of the qualifying regionals, and the freshman and sophomore high school girls were finishing their free skating dance competition when I sat down. The girls' costumes were similar to those we see on ice skaters—Olympic ice skaters, on

TV—sequined leotards over tan-colored tights, but these girls weren't professional athletes. Their body shapes and sizes ran the gamut from what normal folks consider "average" to "chunky."

One obvious difference between quad figure skating and ice skating is that quad roller skates are *heavy*. They are chunky, themselves, so when these girls tried to perform jumps and twirls, they were denied the gravity-defying grace allowed by a 4-millimeter steel blade and slick ice. The freshman and sophomore girls barely managed to lift a few inches off the floor, all the while their faces looking stressed and strained. There was never any illusion of them flying.

After about ten minutes of watching the girls, I spotted Robert and he spotted me and rolled my direction. He was wearing a purple sequined bolero jacket, a tuxedo shirt, black pants, and a bow tie.

"You should meet Bill Duncan," he said, pointing to the silver-haired man sitting in front of me. "He knows everything there is to know about this sport." Robert introduced us, then rolled away to warm up for his qualifying dance.

"You're a writer?" Bill asked. "I'm not much of a writer. I like Bugs Bunny words."

"Like Albuquerque?" I asked.

"That's a good one!" he said.

Bill was both relaxed and alert, wearing a gray houndstooth jacket, a light blue oxford shirt, and super shiny black loafers. His speaking manner was enthusiastic and amiable, like the Midwesterner he was (originally from Kansas City), and I could have easily been convinced to buy insurance or real estate or a dozen farm fresh eggs from him. Bill was a retired skating teacher and competitive roller skater, having gone to Nationals several times. That was the purpose of this day's meet, to decide which skaters would proceed to the national competition. Nationals are held in a different location every year: Lincoln, Nebraska; Peoria, Illinois; Omaha, Nebraska, and in a weird break from the heartland, once in Albuquerque. This year Nationals would be contested in Fort Wayne, Indiana, from July 22—August 7, when I assumed it would be brutally humid.

"So, you know Robert, huh?" Bill said. "We call him Professor Robert, since he's a teacher." I later learned that Robert has a PhD in philosophy from Duke University, then got involved in film studies. He has worked for *The New York Times* and Lincoln Center, and teaches at a small university on the outskirts of Portland—none of which synced up with the purple sequined bolero jacket.

Bill looked around. "So, what do you think of all this?"

"Everyone seems to know each other," I said, watching folks cross the room to talk to each other—some rolling, some walking—all with smiles and laughter. "It's very friendly."

"Oh, sure," Bill said. "This is a middle-class family event. You need *some* money to take lessons and buy skates and travel on the amateur circuit, but you don't need the sort of cash you'd need to participate in, say, golf."

Nationwide, competitive roller skaters live in households with an average income of $41,000-$60,000 and a family of five, firmly ensconcing them in the middle class. The cost of competitive skating totals about $3,500 a year, and—here's the kicker—winning yields *no cash prize.* Just a nice plaque for the winner's skating club. To help offset expenses, family members at Oaks Park sold ham and cheese sandwiches wrapped in cellophane, Rice Krispy squares, giant blueberry muffins, bags of Fritos, and homemade potato salad on a folding table at the front of the skating rink. The potato salad was fifty cents per portion.

Robert was competing in the Golden Men's Solo Dance Final. "Golden" means the competitors were "of a certain age," although asking around (including encyclopedic Bill) yielded no definite answer on what that certain age *is.* All the Golden Men were wearing sequined bolero jackets over tuxedo shirts with bow ties, and pressed black pants. They're scored on, among other things, the neatness of their appearance, so the men were clean-shaven with their gray (or not-so-conspicuously dyed) hair slicked back and up, some veering dangerously close to a shiny pompadour. They stood erect, whether on the rink or off.

These guys took Men's Solo Dance very seriously.

There are two misnomers about this title: One, although it's billed as "Solo Dance," the skaters danced in twos. Not pairs, per se, but they performed their routines—their "flights"—simultaneously, steering respectfully clear of each other on the rink. Two, they weren't dancing. There were no leaps or hops or turns or twirls. They were simply *skating*. The men glided forward in what Bill called a "center lobe pattern," which basically looked like a big spiral. With their bodies tall, arms out to their sides—some looking like eagles ready to take flight—they skated as smoothly as they could, as in rhythm to the music as they could (called "skating in phrase"). I was disappointed there were no acrobatics. It's what I'd hoped for, a moment where Robert and his compadres defied physics and suspended their bodies in space and time.

"Timing is the biggest issue," Bill told me. "Body timing, feet timing, and strike timing." Then he turned to me and asked, "Hey, did I tell you we're going to Copenhagen this summer?"

It's worth noting that Bill and I had known each other for all of five minutes. I said no, he hadn't told me this, and he asked if I'd ever been to Europe. I told him I spent a summer in Florence before my senior year of college, more than twenty years ago.

"I stayed in this crazy hotel in Rome once," he said. "It had a king bed, and the room was exactly the size of a king bed. You had to crawl over it to get to the bathroom."

The music accompanying the flights of two alternated between an organ and accordion recording of "City Blues" with a polka beat, and an organ/accordion recording of "Tara Tango," with a polka beat. The two songs were virtually indistinguishable and eerily reminiscent of the carousel scene at the end of *Strangers on a Train*. The music for all regions is mandated by USA Roller Sports, the governing body in Lincoln, Nebraska. That means that across the country, from California to Connecticut, from Michigan to Mississippi, from Ohio to Oregon, a bevy of senior citizens were all skating to the same creepy polka music in a 2/4 beat on the very same day. Knowing this gave the event a kind of authority and importance—which should not be confused with relevance. It was, according to Bill, a dying sport.

"The biggest mistake our sport has made is not reaching out enough to young people," he said. "Look at the age of most people here."

With the exception of those gravity-bound freshman and sophomore girls, most of the participants seemed to be in their golden years (and, yes—even the golden-aged women were wearing flesh-colored tights and caked-on frosted blue eye shadow). I originally assumed the older crowd was due to the specific age group competing that day, but Bill said kids just didn't find roller skating interesting anymore.

When I was a kid, I loved lacing up the pristine white quad skates my parents had given me for Christmas. I spent my weekends at Skate City, gliding and grooving to the Village People, hoping a foxy guy would ask me to couple-skate (*How Deep Is Your Love?*), and straining my thighs and lungs during speed skate. But when was the last time I did that? When I was thirteen. I never even skated *ironically* in the 1990s.

"What do you think the keys are to getting young people interested?" I asked, as if I was an actual reporter, instead of just a random bystander with a pen.

"Hmmm … I don't know," Bill said. "That's a really good question. I'll have to think about that one," and he looked back to the rink. How had he not considered this before? It seemed it would be a question raised at every committee meeting (did they even have committee meetings?). It made me wonder if Darwinism would win out over roller skating, if the skaters, themselves, were not interested enough in their own survival to adapt and move forward in our short-attention span, instant-gratification, virtual world.

Finally, it was Robert's turn to compete. He took the rink for his flight with a short man as stiff as a mannequin. Skating appeared entirely painful to this pinched little guy, like he'd just gotten a vasectomy. Robert, on the other hand, smiled serenely—a bit like he had a secret, and his secret was that he could take flight anytime he wanted.

Although the rink's wooden floorboards are laid in a curved pattern following the oblong shape of the rink, and although the competitors were skating this counterclockwise "center lobe" spiral, Bill told me that they actually skated from point to point, not in curves. It was a visual trick where the shape of the rink and the smoothness of their lines made it appear as if the skaters were gliding along a dreamy hyperbola.

"He met Bette Davis once." Bill pointed to Robert. "Did you ever see that episode of *Perry Mason* that she was on? The setup was that Perry was out of town, and she took over his practice. Hey, did I tell you we're going to Copenhagen this summer?"

Up until this point, Bill had seemed mostly "with it"—not confused or uncertain or particularly daffy. I thought about my departed dad, who could be a savant about real estate transactions and recalling who played defensive tackle for Notre Dame in 1969, but couldn't figure out how to order a sandwich at the deli or remember to call me on my birthday. It's not that he had dementia, either; it's how he catalogued what was important.

I tried to look surprised by Bill's question and said, "No, that sounds great." Then he asked if I'd ever been to Europe. When I said Italy, he told me about a Roman hotel he stayed in where the room was completely filled by a king bed.

I wasn't aware of what happened next on the rink because it was too subtle, too swift, for my untrained eye and ear. Robert and the mannequin guy finished their flight, exited the floor, and Bill told me, "He was disqualified."

"Who?"

"Professor Robert," he said. "The next skaters were already coming on the floor, and he wasn't off yet. That automatically disqualifies him."

If this did occur, it was only a short overlap, a matter of a couple of feet or seconds, far from the new skaters and not at all interfering with their flight. The disqualification seemed oddly cut-throat, but the rules clearly state that a skater has no more than fifteen seconds to exit the floor after completion of their program. Fifteen seconds *does* seem like ample time to get off the floor, but I had no sense of Robert dawdling. When he skated over to me, I asked him what happened.

"Officially they say I got off the floor too slowly," he said. "But it's all political. That guy wins at *everything*. The judges just love him."

"Him?" I said. "He's so stiff."

Robert shrugged. "The judges like the control."

The word of Robert's disqualification spread quickly, whispered about in the bleachers and in the bathrooms and by the potato salad. I suspected it was the closest this event could ever come to scandal, much less tragedy. The scene inside Oaks Park wasn't so much frozen in a specific era, but a specific moment, where everyone was healthy and whole and the stakes were low and all that was expected of their heads and hearts was skating in phrase to a 2/4 beat.

The awards were handed out for Golden Men's Solo Dance: gold, silver, bronze, plus one qualifier who would also attend Nationals in Fort Wayne. The winners' picture was taken on a makeshift award podium that looked ready to collapse at any second. Robert was disappointed, but not desolate, about his disqualification, because he still had one more event to compete in—the Esquire B Solo Dance—giving him another chance to travel to Fort Wayne.

It never occurred to me to ask what happened after that, after Fort Wayne.

✢

What would this same event look like in New Zealand, or Brazil, or Chinese Taipei? When Worlds are held in Buenos Aires, does the "Tara Tango" actually sound like a tango, or is it still a creepy tango/polka hybrid? What about when they're staged in Reus, Spain, the birthplace of Antoni Gaudí Does the roller rink have a wavy rooftop and lollipop turrets and a colorful mosaic salamander guarding the door? When the championships are in Taiwan, do family members sell Meinong rice noodles and mochi bars with black sesame seeds and xian dou jiang to raise funds? What if it turns out that roller skating isn't an iconically American sport after all, but World Champions more often hail from Italy, and the Federation for International Roller Sports is headquartered in Rome? That in Auckland and Brasília and Wuppertal and Murcia and Portimão the skaters are athletic and lithe, their gossamer georgette and lace leotards ornamented by Swarovski crystals, the music crisp with classical piano and Chinese flutes, the wood floors polished so bright they glisten like ice, and, somehow, gravity is more forgiving in these international locales, because the World Champions are not bound to the ground like they are in Portland, Oregon, but instead they are able to—however fleetingly—take flight.

✛

"You know, I'm old enough that a student of mine has actually died," Bill said. He taught her to skate when she was seven, eight, nine years old. She was full of energy and promise, he said, but when she got older, she started doing drugs. He'd gotten the call just a few days earlier that she'd died of a heart attack at thirty-five. "Can drugs do that to your heart?"

"Sure," I said. "They're hard on the system."

"Cocaine?" he asked.

"Speeds your heart up. Can put you in tachycardia."

"What about heroin?" Bill asked. "What does that do?"

"Slows it way down." My forty-five-year-old brother had already overdosed several times, although on prescription drugs, just like the means of my dad's numerous suicide attempts. I knew none of that made me an expert in pharmacology, but I felt it had made me an expert in something about how life—how promise and love—can so suddenly die.

"That guy always places first." Bill pointed to the gold medal winner. "It helps to be six-foot-four. It makes everything you do look smoother."

I was deciding whether I'd hang around another hour to watch Robert compete in the final event of the day. If he did medal—if he went to Fort Wayne—would I go, too? To see how big a national version of this competition was? To see if it was brighter, more sparkly, more cut-throat, less sincere? To see if, halfway across the country, I could still be suspended in time?

An announcement came over the loudspeaker. "Ladies and gentlemen, there's still lots of food for sale," said a woman I hoped was named Norma. "The potato salad is delicious, and the price has just been reduced to twenty-five cents. We'd hate for food to go to waste."

"Hey, did you know that Professor Robert once met Bette Davis?" Bill asked me.

"It was Barbara Stanwyck," his wife said from the seat in front of him.

"This is my wife." Bill pointed to the younger—but not scandalously so—woman who he'd already introduced me to twice. "Are you sure?"

"I'm sure," she said. "It was Barbara Stanwyck."

Bill looked back to me. "Hey, did I tell you we're going to Copenhagen this summer?"

"I think you mentioned that," I said.

He gazed onto the empty wood floor, void of creepy polka beats. "I bet it's easy to get drugs there."

Maybe skating's problem wasn't so much about getting young people involved, but keeping them involved. Plenty of kids—especially girls—skated. And plenty of senior citizens seemed to, too. But it's that place in between, that place called adulthood, where the sport lost its acolytes. Where we all lose faith in the illusion that joy can be captured, even for an hour, by strapping wheels to our feet and moving faster and smoother than we do in real life. The scene at Oaks Park gave me a small hope that maybe, when I reached a certain age, I would be able to reclaim my belief in that unencumbered joy.

I decided not to wait another hour to watch Robert skate again. I went to the bathroom, and then walked straight to the exit so I wouldn't have to navigate the awkwardness I always feel in saying goodbye. When I stepped outside, the afternoon sunlight had grown oddly diffuse, but the midway was still deserted. The Ferris wheel was dormant, and the demonic horses remained frozen in place. And so I beat on against the banks of the Willamette, a boat against the current, borne back ceaselessly into the past.

Magnum Force

A helicopter soars past Waikīkī Beach, bare-chested Thomas Magnum shoves a clip into his .45 caliber pistol, a yellow car bursts into flames, Magnum holds a prone woman afloat in the Pacific as he stares at her bikini-clad ass, a red Ferrari speeds down the Kamehameha Highway, Tom Selleck looks over his shoulder and raises his eyebrows with a smirk.

I picture my brother Steve watching all this. He's lying belly down on our dad's bed, his chin propped up by one hand. He's sixteen, seventeen, eighteen—years away from his too-early death at the age of forty-five—and his six-foot-four body is still muscular. Steve wears blue gym shorts, a blue and white aloha shirt, and a Detroit Tigers baseball cap. He's growing a mustache that's filling in strong.

Steve never missed an episode of *Magnum, P.I.*, never missed a repeat, kept episodes on videotape so he could watch them again and again. *Magnum, P.I.* premiered on December 11, 1980, three days after his fifteenth birthday. That age, fifteen, is when my mom and dad and I later agreed that Steve's drinking problem started, when his sudden inability to fit into his own social and athletic world erupted and when—I now know—the first signs of bipolar disorder often appear. If I could go back in time, I'd watch my brother watching. I'd try to see what he saw in Thomas Magnum that he so badly wanted to emulate.

Magnum, P.I. was a fun show, with car chases and gun fights, pretty shots of Hawaiian beaches and palm trees, all peppered with Magnum's self-deprecating sense of humor. His buddy, Rick, owned an exclusive beach bar, and pal T.C., reluctantly provided his helicopter to aid in the solving of Magnum's cases. His friends were constantly annoyed by Magnum's dependence on them and their resources, but they ultimately had his back.

The pilot episode was a two-hour movie that begins with Magnum swimming in the Pacific, with a verdant Hawaiian cliffside as the backdrop. He steps foot on the beach and runs along a sea wall, carrying a mysterious plastic bag. In voice over, Tom Selleck says: "It's funny, the things a grown man will do for a living. Especially me. Take this morning: I'm breaking into Robin Masters' estate. You know, the writer? The one with all those best sellers?" And then he says wistfully: "All that money."

Robin Masters doesn't live at "Robin's Nest," his estate on O'ahu— he just flies in once or twice a year—but allows his friends to spend time there. Higgins, an uptight, former British military officer who is the keeper of the manor, resolutely believes Robin's Nest is an impenetrable fort. Magnum, in exchange for living free in the guest house and driving Robin's candy red Ferrari, stages a series of break-in attempts to test Higgins' belief. Magnum gets to sleep in, hang out at Rick's beach bar, and drive a snazzy car provided by the owner of the house. Despite his apparent envy of Robin's financial means, it would appear that Magnum has very little need for money of his own.

My brother also concocted a lifestyle that required him to earn very little money of his own. For the majority of Steve's adult life, he lived with our dad, Pete, rent free with a car bought by our dad. He "worked for" Pete in real estate, but rarely had to report to an office and often slept until noon. I wonder if Steve got the idea from *Magnum* that it would be cool, somehow, to live on someone else's dime—to enjoy the freedoms of being an adult, without any of the responsibilities.

But *Magnum, P.I.* quickly establishes that Thomas *earned* his carefree lifestyle. While still crouched along the seawall, Selleck says, "Like I said … funny, the things a grown man will do for a living." The camera zooms in on a ring decorated with a French cross, his hand rubbing his scar-laced shoulder. "But I've done funnier."

The scene dissolves into a black-and-white quick-cut montage: beret-wearing military men shooting machine guns in the jungle, Magnum carrying a wounded soldier across his shoulders amid a hail of shrapnel while another man falls at his feet, a commander who'd taken Magnum's gun shooting toward the unseen enemy, T.C. setting his helicopter down in a precarious clearing so Magnum can board, the commander being mortally shot, the chopper fleeing to the sky.

The scene returns to present, to color, to Magnum in the paradise that is Hawai'i. In that seven-second PTSD flashback we learn that Magnum and his friends were once men of honor. They were highly skilled and believed in what they were doing. But, like many Vietnam vets, they became disillusioned. They witnessed brutality they'd never been exposed to before, especially in themselves. They are forever bound by loyalty to the men with whom they served, but are suspicious of the government *for* whom they served.

A decade later in Honolulu, Magnum and his pals aren't living the lives of normal thirty-three-year-olds: none of them are married or have children, work for anyone else, or have to report to an office. They are resolute on grabbing their lost youth back from the jaws of war.

Magnum and his friends' tours and trauma in Vietnam is more than just a minor thread in the series, it is *the* thread holding all the others in place. Over eight seasons, plotlines return to it again and again. It's not as if a dedicated viewer like my brother could have, somehow, glossed over this part. But in my experience, Steve was not someone who embraced darkness. His uniform was colorful Polo shirts and dark blue jeans. He sang along to light-hearted pop music and Rat Pack standards. He could recite all the lines from Chevy Chase movies.

Deep, philosophical conversations about love and death never sat on his lips. Even after our mom died when Steve was 28 and I was 26, he didn't want to talk about the loss, about our shared grief. I don't know if my brother gravitated to *Magnum, P.I.* because the tropical lightness allowed him to temporarily escape the growing torment in his own brain, or because threads of it actually reflected the fear, isolation, and paranoia within his fractured psyche.

✢

By the spring of 2009, my dad and brother were mired in dire physical and psychiatric straits. My brother had been hit by the triple whammy of untreated mental illness, vascular necrosis that destroyed his hip sockets, and our dad's inability to steer him in a healthy way. All Steve needed to be pain-free was to have both his hips replaced. Total hip replacement is a relatively safe surgery, with mortality rates ranging from .3% to .65% and occurring almost exclusively in people over the age of 70. My brother was forty-one when the procedure was first recommended for him. Yet he and my dad were both so beset with anxiety and certainty that Steve would die, they decided against the surgery. Whatever input I offered that bended towards "reason" was brushed aside. Pete convinced Steve to try alternative methods—which largely included some contraption a quack from the Midwest claimed would heal any and everything. Guess what? It didn't. There is no secret cure for the disintegration of your bones.

My brother's pain intensified. He needed a walker to navigate the top floor of their house. He gulped down prescription morphine and oxycodone. But his hips were bone on bone. He sat in a medical recliner most of the day. The lack of mobility caused his legs to swell to twice their size, and infections ravaged his skin. He added Xanax and Ambien and whiskey and beer to his opioids. The cornucopia of pills was prescribed by five different doctors—including ones in Los

Angeles, King of Prussia and Philadelphia, P.A., and Puerto Rico—and filled by three different pharmacies, including the local Walgreens and The Meetinghouse Community Pharmacy, which was closed by the DEA in 2009 for providing mail-order distribution of controlled substances.

Steve was unable to get out of bed, unable to sit up, and laid horizontal for months on end. He lost muscle, but didn't waste away. Fat billowed around his body, creating another buffer between his fragile insides and the harsh outside world. The only time he left the house was when EMTs wheeled him out because of an overdose or life-threatening infection.

It took a toll on our eighty-year-old dad. He hired "caregivers" (scare-quotes intentional), who let Steve take as many pills as he wanted, whenever he wanted. They constantly screamed at Steve and Pete, and threatened to abandon them. "If we leave, who will take care of you?" they'd yell. "No one!" Between Steve's uninsured pill habit and the circus of caregivers, his medical care was costing nearly $10,000 per month. Pete was desperate and panicked and swallowing his own fair share of Ambien and Xanax. In phone call after phone call, he told me, "Every night I pray, *take me, Lord.*"

I tried to convince him to see a therapist. He tried to get me to move from Portland to Denver so I could be the one to dress and kiss their blistering wounds. I encouraged him to move Steve to a skilled nursing facility. He said he'd never abandon his son like that. I coaxed him to hire new caregivers. My dad tried to kill himself.

He didn't take enough pills to complete the task. He didn't even take enough for the hospital to take it seriously—not the first time, at least. "Sometimes old people forget how many pills they've taken," the nurse told me, even though I relayed his desire to die. After seventy-two hours, the hospital sent him home.

Four days later, my dad signed the papers for a reverse mortgage on my childhood home.

✝

"You've probably been investing in your home for years, making monthly mortgage payments, doing the right thing, and it's become your family's heart and soul."

Tom Selleck is seventy-four years old the first time I see him in a commercial for American Advisers Group. He "looks good" for his age, meaning he appears to dye his hair and is a little jowly, but at least he has hair (including his trademark mustache), and is in good enough health to star on the CBS drama *Blue Bloods*. When he speaks, it isn't with the upbeat lilt of Thomas Magnum, but with a calm, folksy resonance. At least, that's the persona he uses in the ads promoting reverse mortgages that started airing six, seven years after my dad and brother died.

Throughout the two-minute ad, Selleck ambles from one bucolic scene to another—from a rolling pasture, to a tree lined road, to a wood cattle fence. He's wearing a light blue plaid cotton shirt and a camel suede jacket, unzipped.

"Look, this isn't my first rodeo," he says. "And let me tell you something: I wouldn't be here if I thought reverse mortgages took advantage of *any* American senior or, worse, that it was some way to take your home."

Selleck talks to the viewer casually but seriously, reassuringly waving his hands and shrugging in a golly-gee sort of way. You can trust him, is what all this is designed to convey. AAG's previous spokesperson, Fred Thompson, had also ambled across grass and leaned on ranch fences. Thompson was a former Republican Senator from Tennessee, and an actor whose roles were often those of a district attorney or judge or sheriff. He was an old white man who'd portrayed or held positions of power in the vanguard of old white men. The Greatest Generation cohort found him trustworthy.

But after Thompson died and *USA Today* published a scathing exposé on the devastating impact of shady reverse mortgages, the industry realized that seniors weren't the only demographic who needed to be sold. The younger heirs who might be consulted in decision making, who might seek solutions to keep their beloved childhood home, had to believe in reverse mortgages, too. AAG conducted extensive research to find the right celebrity spokesperson, asking consumer focus groups questions like, "If you could choose one celebrity to have over as a dinner guest, who would you invite?" and "Who do you think best represents your age group?" Their research showed that Selleck garnered "widespread recognition and respect across generations."

AAG's research explains why they wanted Selleck, but not why Selleck took the job. Selleck was already making a pretty good living at $150,000 per episode of *Blue Bloods*, with a net worth around $45 million. In an AAG press release, Selleck is quoted as saying that it was Thompson who "sparked" his interest in reverse mortgages, and that he thinks it's important "for many Americans 62 and older" to know the benefits of a reverse mortgage. Like everything else Selleck gets paid for, it's obvious that he's adhering to a script.

I guess it *is* funny the things a grown man will do for a living.

"A reverse mortgage loan isn't some kind of trick to take your home," Selleck says. "It's a loan, like any other loan. Big difference is in how you pay it back."

The word "trick" implies a certain silly/paranoid level of conspiracy theory behind all the reverse mortgage naysayers (like the Consumer Financial Protection Bureau, for instance). After all, Selleck says, it's just a loan—except that it's not *exactly* a loan like any other loan. A reverse mortgage (aka: a home equity conversion mortgage, aka: a HECM) is based solely on the equity in your house. The reverse mortgage company (the lender) appraises the value of your house, and you can borrow against that amount. The percentage of the total equity you can borrow has fluctuated over the years, but has never been more than 80%.

"Other mortgages are paid each month," Selleck says, "but with a reverse mortgage you can pay whatever you can, when it works for you. Or you can wait and pay it off in one lump sum when you leave your home."

Generally, seniors leave their homes because they require more care (i.e., assisted living) or because they're going out feet first. Assisted living costs between $4,000–$8,000 a month, depending on the level of care. But wait! The senior *first* has to pay back the HECM they borrowed however many years ago, the one that would allow them to stay in their home and pass it on to their kids.

The majority of seniors who take out HECMs do so because they need money for health care, home maintenance, and basic living costs. Assuming they've been using the loan for those purposes, they probably don't have a lot of extra dough lying around to pay it back *and* finance the next step in their life—especially since reverse mortgages often come with hefty compounding interest rates and service fees. My dad's reverse mortgage accrued $33,000 a year in interest alone.

If the senior leaves their home toe-up, then the entire loan balance is due immediately. That's fairly unrealistic, because a deceased person's accounts are often frozen as the estate goes through testate or probate, and money can't be distributed until it's settled. Knowing this, most HECM lenders allow heirs to take out extensions on the due date, during which time interest *continues to accrue*. If, when all is settled, the estate has enough funds to repay the loan, then cool. The heirs can do whatever they want with the house—keep it, sell it, split the profit.

If the estate doesn't have enough funds to pay off the loan, the heirs have the option of selling the home and repaying the HECM with the proceeds. This all goes horribly sideways if the lender over-inflated the value of the house for the basis of the loan, and there's no feasible way for the heirs to sell it for that much. That's when "your family's heart and soul" goes into foreclosure.

✛

There are many, many details I don't know or understand about the demise of my dad and brother—mostly because they kept realities from me, or told outright lies. I don't think they were trying to protect me, the youngest, the girl, from hard truths. I think they were trying to protect themselves, convince themselves, convince anyone who would listen that they hadn't really fucked up as badly as they had. But the gnarliest knot I had to unkink was my dad's financial situation.

Pete had once been a well-off man, a rags-to-riches son of poor immigrants, who eventually made millions through shrewd purchases of land. But just as my dad could be smart when looking at acreage, he'd be equally as foolish in choosing business partners. He was blinded by flash and big talk, even before old age, and lost money to more than one snake oil salesman. By the time he was elderly and his son was disabled, he suffered from desperation and slight dementia and a propensity to solve problems with prescription sedatives. Somehow, by spring 2009, Pete's liquidity had dwindled to having about eighteen months of living expenses for him and Steve.

I don't know how the reverse mortgage idea came to him, because I didn't know about the reverse mortgage until it was too late to ask. Here's what I do know: HECM companies advertise around shows like *Wheel of Fortune*, *M*A*S*H* re-runs, and odd-houred cable news shows. Back in the 2000s, brokers peddling HECMs also placed hangers on doorknobs and sent out junk mail. The envelope would say in big PAY ATTENTION TO ME lettering that inside was a *Notice of Government Benefits* (um, not true). The fliers promised seniors a "risk-free/tax-free" way to access the equity in their home, so they could stay in it as long as they wanted (also not true). All they had to do was call this 1-800 number *now*.

It's easy to imagine my desperate dad seeing one of these TV ads, finding one of these fliers on his door, opening a piece of mail, and saying, "Yes, this is what will save me and my son." So, he spoke to a broker at Reverse Mortgage Solutions (RMS).

According to the Consumer Financial Protection Bureau, RMS routinely told potential customers they needed to sign by the end of the day, or the company would "turn your file down and you will miss out on a tremendous money-saving opportunity." One of the few clues I found about how, exactly, my dad signed this shifty reverse mortgage came from his attorney, after both he and my brother died. The attorney said Pete had called him about the loan, saying, "I think I made a big mistake." The attorney looked over the paperwork, agreed it was a big mistake, but found a loophole—a three-day look period—and helped my dad back out. Whew, my dad was safe!

Except he wasn't. Because his financial desperation hadn't been cured, nor his suicidal depression, nor his mentally and physically disabled, drug-addicted son. More than that, there was nothing protecting him from follow-up phone calls from Reverse Mortgage Solutions saying things along the lines of, "Are you sure? Listen, I promise this is risk-free. If you act now, you still have a chance to get this money." *You can still be saved.* So, Pete once again signed on the dotted line—and this time didn't back out.

The lump sum granted was $485,000—supposedly 80% of the value of his home. Full draw/lump sum loans are no longer allowed, precisely because the low, *low* chance of them being repaid led to mass foreclosures. The magical thinking behind a lump sum loan was that the home value would appreciate, so it would be easy-peasy to pay back! In reality, reverse mortgage lenders had this annoying (and by "annoying," I mean "hugely unethical") tendency to over-inflate the value of the property, and balances due usually far exceeded the market value.

My dad applied for a HECM only six months after the financial collapse of 2008. This was precisely when the Denver real estate bubble burst and home prices were at their absolute lowest. Yet, RMS appraised Pete's house at $572,000. Okay, sure, it was four-thousand square feet, but the kitchen hadn't been updated in over twenty years and the bathrooms hadn't been updated since it was built in 1966. The house was also in a neighborhood where the average home went for $300,000–$380,000. There was no possible way his house was worth $572,000.

The average term of a reverse mortgage is seven years, which I suppose is theoretically long enough for the market to bounce back and a home to appreciate. But Pete was 82 when he took out the loan. The average life expectancy of a male in the U.S. was 78.5 years. I'm not a mathematical or statistical genius by any stretch of the imagination, but even I can spot the problematic gap between the average life expectancy, and seven years past the age when my dad took out the loan. There would never be enough time for the house to appreciate.

✜

My dad died in June 2010, fourteen months after taking out the reverse mortgage. Both my parents were dead. I was forty-three, so it's not like I was some Dickensian foundling forced to live on the street, but I felt orphaned, alone, nonetheless. I flew to Denver and went straight to my family home, where my brother lay flat in his hospital bed. We cried and I kissed his soft cheek. Steve looked me directly in the eyes. "We'll make all the decisions together," he said. "It's just you and me, Sis."

But Steve was so physically and emotionally disabled, so constantly lost in an opiate haze, I had to make and pay for all the funeral arrangements. I had to figure out what to do about this damn reverse mortgage due as soon as the borrower dies. We didn't just owe the principal amount, but also an additional $45,000 in interest and processing fees—bringing the amount due to a grand total of $530,000.

The only way to sell the house quickly enough to repay the loan would be a "fire sale" at a drastically reduced price, and I guess combine the funds with the remainder of my dad's estate. Small problem: It turned out my dad's estate was surprisingly paltry. He died with a lot of debt and very little cash. The remainder of the lump sum he'd received from RMS was nowhere to be found, and Pete's bankers and lawyers and accountants couldn't find even a breadcrumb of a trail as to where the money had gone. We were extra screwed because Steve was living in the house with 24/7 live-in care. There was no money to move him to an assisted care facility. Plus, he wanted to stay in our childhood home.

"I'm going to find a way to save the house," Steve told me on the phone in the months after our dad died. We took out two 180-day extensions on the loan (while $3,000 per month in interest and vague "service fees" continued to accrue), but I knew there was no way to pay it off. Over a half-million dollars wasn't suddenly going to drop out of the sky. The house would go into foreclosure and be repossessed by the bank. So, the question became: Where would Steve go?

Steve went the only path he could have gone, given the circumstances of his life. A few months after our dad died, a severe overdose sent him to the hospital. He briefly tried to stop abusing drugs and alcohol and attempted physical rehab. But his mental illness—and enormous grief—wasn't addressed, and he eventually retreated to drugs and drinking, to overdoses and infections. To his bed.

My brother died in his sleep on August 29, 2011, somewhere around three or four in the morning. He'd just gotten out of the hospital for another overdose, another infection, but it wasn't another overdose or infection that killed him. It was two unpredictable pulmonary emboli. After his funeral, his friends and my friends went to a bar for a wake. We were eating Irish Nachos—potato chips covered in tender corned beef and cheese and green onions—when my friend Marie asked me what was going to happen to the house.

"Officially, it went into foreclosure on the one-year anniversary of Pete's death," I said, which was three months earlier. "But I can't find any official documents saying when we have to be out by."

"When our condo was foreclosed on, we just came home one day and there was a sign on the door saying we have forty-eight hours to clear the premises," Marie said. "Then they change the locks and board it up. Anything left behind they sell or throw away."

Living a thousand miles away, I wouldn't see some official notice taped to the door. And even if a local friend stopped by the house every single day just to check whether or not the death knell sign was posted, how could I possibly scramble to Denver in enough time to clean out that enormous house in forty-eight hours? Everything, *everything* from cradle to grave would get sold to strangers or thrown away.

I needed to come back to Denver soon so I could make those decisions for myself: what to keep, what to throw away, what to sell, what to shred. Three weeks after Steve's funeral, I returned to Denver with my husband and, with the help of a half-dozen intrepid friends, set out to clean a 4,000-square-foot house that had been occupied by two small-time hoarders for forty-five years. Keep, throw away, give away, shred, was the mantra for every object in every room.

Steve had three bedrooms in the house. His "adult" bedroom was upstairs, in what we always called The New Addition, even though it had been built onto the house in 1984. By 2009, the increasing frequency with which EMTs had to haul Steve's 400-pound body downstairs prompted his move into my dad's downstairs study. Pete's shiny oval desk and plaid club chairs were pushed into a corner of the garage, and Steve's hospital bed was wheeled in.

His first bedroom, the one from his childhood, was forever frozen in time: the mustard yellow bedspread on his twin bed, a closet full of old sports uniforms, plastic Army men and Matchbook cars, bookshelves lined with gold and silver-toned trophies (basketball, baseball, football, bowling), and a Detroit Tigers baseball cap. The wallpaper was a muddy cacophony of avocado green and gold, on top of which hung posters from Steve's teen years: Farrah Fawcett in a red one-piece bathing suit, Daisy Duke in a gingham top and cut-off shorts, and Tom Selleck sitting in a red Ferrari as trademark character, Thomas Magnum.

I cleaned out the house several years before Tom Selleck was reassuring folks that reverse mortgages aren't some way to take your home, and if he trusted reverse mortgages then "you can, too." I experienced no immediate sense of irony upon seeing the Magnum poster hanging in my brother's bedroom as I desperately prepared the house for foreclosure. The link between that poster and Tom Selleck ambling down pastoral roads makes one thing perfectly clear, though: there was no way I could have saved my childhood home from the swindle of a reverse mortgage, no way I could have saved my dad and brother from the bad choices born from their mental illnesses.

Even if the federal government had investigated and fined Reverse Mortgage Solutions and their ilk before Steve and Pete died, even if the scathing media exposés had come five years earlier, it still would have been too late to save my family. See, that's the reason AAG hires celebrities as their spokespeople, whether it's Fred Thompson or Tom Selleck. "When [retirees] see a celebrity, it's like, 'There's a life raft,'" said a gerontologist interviewed by *The New York Times*. "'I've got problems, and Tom Selleck … represents someone who has solutions.'"

My brother's hero, the person he wanted to be—or, at least, the actor who played him—would have calmly assured my brother that a reverse mortgage would preserve the walls and furniture and everyday objects that provided his sense of safety. Fred Thompson probably reassured my dad. There would always have been someone Pete and Steve believed had easy answers to their complex problems.

In October of 2011, after a harrowing four days of keep, throw away, give away, shred, I closed the door to the house I grew up in for the last time. The bank repossessed it, and eventually sold it for $330,000. Coincidentally, in 2015 the estate used for Robin's Nest in *Magnum, P.I.* was sold for half its asking price, and was demolished in 2018. The estate is still a pile of rubble.

Amid my own rubble is a photograph of Steve standing at the gate of Robin's Nest. His six-foot-four body is muscular, his brown mustache filled in. He wears blue gym shorts, a blue and white aloha shirt, and a Detroit Tigers baseball cap. He looks happy, smiling, exactly where he wants to be. Over his right shoulder is a stone sign that says "Pahonu," the real-life name of the estate used for filming *Magnum, P.I.* On the show, Robin's Nest was a 200-acre estate located on Kalakaua Street on O'ahu's North Shore. In real life, Pahonu is three acres on the Southeast side of the island. I'm sure these inconsistencies didn't bother Steve, as he knew certain fictions are necessary to build illusion.

To Steve's left is a sign that says, "Do Not Climb on Gate or Rock Wall. Do Not Destroy the Plants. Please Respect Private Property." The sign hangs on a locked wrought iron gate, begging my brother to stay outside.

Falling Off Radar

The bar of Chili's was crammed with Denver suburbanites in the waning days of 1988. A neon chili pepper made everything glow red: carpet, bar stools, air, flesh. I was home from college on winter break, and my dad and I were waiting for a table on this twelve-degree night. I spotted my friend, Annie, sitting on a barstool next to her mom. We'd met at Kent Denver my sophomore and her freshman year, and immediately bonded over our love of the theater and our mad crushes on two guys in jazz band. She was a good girlfriend to share a crush with because she was a true romantic, always sparkling with the belief that love could conquer all.

After high school, Annie went to college at Syracuse, and I went to Lewis and Clark. She continued with the theater, but I ditched it for boys and weed. When I saw her in Chili's that week between Christmas and New Year's, I hadn't heard from her in at least six months. It didn't mean much back then—nothing personal, especially before the advent of email and texting—no reflection on how we felt about each other. It just meant we were busy with twenty-year-old's lives.

"Ohmygod, Annie!" I squealed and jumped up and down, because we were the kind of girlfriends who made each other squeal and jump up and down.

"Oh," she said, dead-eyed, dead-voiced. "Hi."

I wrapped my arms around her, but she didn't hug back. She was ragdoll-limp, as if nothing was inside. I stepped away and saw her shoulders, heavy and round. Her mouth drooped down, like she had no control of her facial muscles. She didn't look at me, or away.

"Annie," I said. "Are you okay?"

"I was supposed to be on the plane," she said.

"What plane?"

"The one that exploded over Scotland last week," she said, monotone. "All my friends were on it."

✜

On December 21, 1988, Pan Am Flight 103 took off from London's Heathrow airport at 6:25 p.m. en route to JFK. Onboard were 243 passengers and 16 crew members. Of the 179 American passengers, 35 were Syracuse University students who had spent the fall semester studying in London—with Annie. Among those students on the plane were eight of her close friends in the drama program, including her best friend, Theodora Cohen. Just twenty-four hours before takeoff, Annie thought she'd be sitting next to Theo on Flight 103.

Since the previous summer, Annie had been gripped by a new and inexplicable fear of flying. Anxiety attacks sent her to the emergency room, they dropped her to the ground. The only way she could fly to England in the first place was by drinking copious amounts of alcohol. While in London, her dreams were haunted by airplane disasters, a plane cracking in half, an airport engulfed in flames, Annie trying to escape. She was terrified about her flight back to the United States when the study abroad program ended. She was sure she was going to die.

Annie's original plan had been to fly from London to Boston on December 22nd, and then catch a flight to Denver to spend Christmas with her family. Theo urged Annie to fly back with her instead, the day before Annie's scheduled flight. Theo promised she'd hold Annie's hand the entire time and everything would be okay. Annie decided that's what she would do: board Flight 103 on December 21st along with her friends. But it turned out the logistics of getting from JFK to Denver became too complicated, so Annie reverted to her original plan to leave London the day after her friends.

The day her friends left, Annie and Theo ate at their favorite falafel restaurant, joking that the garbanzos and pita was Theo's Last Supper. They returned to their flat so Theo could finish last-minute packing, chatting with three other friends who lived in the building and were also flying out that evening. Theo had forgotten to put an earring in the third hole in her ear, so she asked to borrow one from Annie. As she handed Theo her earring, Annie thought "*this is the last time I'll see that earring*"—because Annie was that certain she would die flying home the next day.

A few hours before their departure, Annie walked her friends downstairs to their cab. Theo gave Annie a big hug, did a theatrical jeté off the steps of their building, and said, "I'll see you soon."

Annie took a long walk, then went back to her flat to watch TV. Just minutes after she turned it on, there was breaking news: a plane had fallen off radar somewhere over Scotland. That was all the media knew at that point, but Annie let out a scream that came from her toes.

✛

I don't remember what I said that night in Chili's when Annie told me her friends were dead. I hope I didn't deliver some lame platitude designed make her feel better … but I probably did. We are all rendered inarticulate when faced with another's loss, and youth makes the banality of platitudes that much more accessible.

Everything else about that night—the neon red, Annie's monotone words, the death in her eyes—haunted me for decades. And it wasn't the lost souls who rattled around my psyche, slamming doors and clanking chains. It was Annie, this friend from my youth. It was loss. It was an alarm bell proclaiming my destiny.

✝

Approximately twenty-seven minutes after takeoff from Heathrow, Scottish air traffic control lost radio contact with Flight 103. Their radar screen showed not just one blip where the plane should be, but five. And then those five blips fanned out and fell off the screen. The blips represented the cockpit, the fuselage, an engine, and each wing hurtling to earth after an explosion tore through the plane.

Investigators concluded that a bomb had detonated from a Samsonite suitcase planted inside the forward baggage hold. The explosion caused the immediate disintegration of the Boeing 747. Emergency procedures were never initiated. All the controls in the cockpit were still set to cruise control. No oxygen masks had dropped down. It's theorized that most of the passengers and crew immediately lost consciousness from severe hypoxia. It's also possible that victims regained consciousness as they spun 31,000 feet towards the earth. It took approximately two minutes for the victims' bodies—and body parts—to fall to the ground in Lockerbie, where another eleven people were killed by fallout.

Those two minutes occupied an exponential amount of time in Annie's mind over the years. She wondered how much her friends knew about what was happening to them, especially since Theo's body hit the ground intact. She hoped they instantly blacked out—and stayed that way. All things considered, losing consciousness was the best-case scenario.

✝

What does it do to a person to lose so many loved ones all at once?

How do you survive? I wondered if Annie was still a romantic, if she still believed love could conquer all. Did she still giggle and talk fast? Was she still passionate about life? Did she still have sparkling eyes? The last time I'd seen her, there was nothing but death in those eyes.

How do you trust, how do you love, how do you move on, how do you live, were some of the questions that haunted me for years.

✛

Annie flew back to the United States the day after Pan Am 103 was struck down. She was so numbed by shock and grief that she couldn't have cared less if she died. For those few hours, Annie no longer feared flying. She was pushed through Heathrow in a wheelchair, but beyond that no special provisions were made for her. No trauma therapist helped her board or fly. She was put in any old seat in the back of the plane.

It wasn't until the pilot learned Annie was a Syracuse student that he arranged to have her moved to first class. He, too, had lost colleagues, friends, in the bombing. I often wonder if he could feel Annie back there, if they were linked by a tether of unbearable pain.

✛

After seeing each other at Chili's, Annie and I wrote a couple of letters and talked on the phone once or twice. I even called her mom to make sure Annie was "doing okay." At twenty, I had no idea how asinine that concept was. I didn't know a thing of PTSD or survivor's guilt or even complex grief, not like I do now. I didn't know how loss changes us, how it twists into our DNA and alters our genetic code.

Two months after seeing each other, I received a letter from Annie written on mint-green stationery with a colorful parrot on top. She said, "I can't tell you how good it was to see you again. I am really sorry it wasn't under better circumstances." She said, "I am hanging in there. I am really busy, which always helps." She told me she'd been seeing a new guy, but he had gotten very serious very quickly. "I don't know if I'm able to be close to anyone right now," she wrote. "Commitment is not in my vocabulary. Help." Annie ended the letter, "Please keep in touch. I have missed you a great deal and don't want to lose contact again." She signed it, "Friends Forever."

We didn't talk for another fifteen years.

✛

The investigation into the bombing of Flight 103 dragged on for over two years. In November of 1991, two Libyan men, Lamin Khalifah Fhimah and Abdel Bassett Ali al-Megrahi were indicted for the murders of 270 people. Fhimah worked for Libyan Arab Airlines in Malta, where the Samsonite suitcase began its journey. Al-Megrahi was a Libyan intelligence officer and a suspected member of Muammar Qaddafi's inner circle. Libya refused to extradite the men to the United States or United Kingdom, since no extradition treaty between the three countries existed. In late 1998, all countries involved finally agreed upon a trial in the Netherlands governed by Scots law. Ten years had passed since the bombing, and still no one had been held accountable.

The trial began in May 2000 and lasted through January 2001. On January 31st, the judges found Lamin Khalifah Fhimah not guilty, and he was immediately freed and allowed to return to Libya. Abdel Bassett Ali al-Megrahi was found guilty of the murder of 270 people. He was sentenced to life imprisonment, with a recommendation that he should serve at least twenty years before being eligible for parole.

I don't remember for sure if it was January 31st, or February 1st— or maybe, with time zones being what they are, if it was January 30th

2001—when I called Annie for the first time in fifteen years. I just know it was the same day I heard the news that the trial had concluded. I looked her up on Google and found her number and called.

She didn't remember who I was.

"We were pretty good friends," I mumbled. "I thought."

Annie stayed on the phone with me. She didn't say, "Hmm, sorry," and hang up—which would have been easy to do. Especially since, in my utter lack of wisdom, I'd chosen to call her on the exact same day the verdicts were announced. All this time I'd been wondering what kind of trauma one endures from such a heinous loss, and yet, in that moment, it didn't occur to me to let that trauma breathe.

As I fed Annie memories of our friendship, others came back to her. I didn't remind her of the last time we'd seen each other, at Chili's. The ground beneath us was tenuous enough. We eventually got to the stuff of regular life: She was living in Seattle, married, had a daughter, and was still acting. We'd both lost our mothers around the same time, in our mid-twenties. We promised to keep in touch. But unlike when the promise was scribbled on mint green stationary to me in 1989, we now had the internet. We had email, and then social media.

On a seemingly random day in August of 2009, Annie posted on Facebook "Flooded with memories of old friends, and miss Theo."

I messaged her and told her what I remembered, and learned what she didn't. She didn't remember seeing me that night at Chili's, or the mint green letter she wrote me a few months later. "I was pretty fried for a couple of years," she said. "So, it doesn't surprise me." I told her that the night at Chili's and the bombing had lodged in my head and viscera for decades. I told her about all the times I tried to make sense of the senseless. And then it occurred to me, here she was, the person and the experience I'd wondered about for years. The source for all the questions I'd ruminated on was virtually in front of me. I asked Annie if I could interview and write about her.

I know it's a lot—very emotional to revisit, no doubt—but it would be my true honor to be your witness.

✝

Although the bombing of Pan Am Flight 103 didn't take place on American soil, Pan Am was an American corporation, the jet originated in the U.S., and the majority of the victims were Americans, so it was classified as an attack against the United States. It was the first time the United States was the victim of a wide-scale terrorist attack. This was before the Oklahoma City bombing, before the Atlanta Olympics, before the two World Trade Center attacks, and before the mass shootings in nightclubs and movie theaters and Walmart and schools.

In 1988, *post-traumatic stress* was mainly a diagnosis for men who had seen combat in the jungles of Vietnam. *Survivor's guilt* was applied to Jewish people who managed to escape Nazi concentration camps while their families were extinguished. Neither terms were commonly applied to upper-middle class college students. Syracuse provided therapists for students who lost friends in the terrorist attack, but they were ill-prepared for the trauma the survivors faced.

Annie believed the nightmares—the premonitions, she called them—she experienced before the bombing were given to her for a reason, and that she had failed by not knowing what to make of them. By not being able to prevent the tragedy. Like Cassandra, Annie had been rendered powerless to her visions. The therapist Annie saw for a good portion of her senior year didn't believe the nightmares were premonitions. She said Annie survivor's guilt was making her believe that she had presaged the tragedy; she even cast doubt on whether Annie's dreams and nightmares ever really occurred at all. That her own therapist, the person tasked with helping Annie heal, didn't believe the underlying cause of Annie's guilt was real, made Annie feel even more crazy.

✛

I interviewed Annie in Seattle, the day after seeing her perform in David Hare's *The Vertical Hour*. The play revolves around four characters discussing politics, terrorism, and the 2003 U.S. invasion of Iraq, over breakfast and dinner and a late-night rendezvous. Annie's role was that of Nadia Blye, an American professor nicknamed "the terrorism expert."

Annie said it was a coincidence, or synchronicity, or a completely subconscious decision to audition for a play that tackles the topic of terrorism so brashly. She said it was "fate" that the show's opening night fell on what would have been Theo's fortieth birthday.

"Terrorism may be the wrong answer to the right question," Annie/Nadia said from the stage of the ArtsWest theater in Seattle, nearly two decades after the attack on Pan Am 103. "The moment at which an individual picks up a gun, or prepares an explosive … that moment is still deeply obscure. People claim to understand it, but do they? I certainly don't."

That truth—that you can never truly understand—tortured Annie for years. "Why?" she constantly asked. "Why them, and not me?" She couldn't reconcile her belief in fate with a cosmic reason for the murder of her friends. Annie finally accepted that she would never understand why she wasn't on that plane, why her friends were. Why Abdel Basset al-Megrahi planted a bomb in the forward baggage hold that day.

"If you don't accept that in some way, in some fashion," she said to me, "how do you move forward?"

✛

On August 20, 2009, Abdel Bassett Ali al-Megrahi was freed from prison. He said he had terminal prostate cancer, with only three months left to live. The Scottish government released him on compassionate grounds. Al-Megrahi served only eight years of what was supposed to be a life sentence for the murder of 270 people: approximately eleven days in jail for every person he murdered. He returned to Libya, greeted by a cheering crowd. The jubilant homecoming sparked international outrage, further fueled by footage of Muammar Qaddafi hugging al-Megrahi and thanking British Prime Minister Gordon Brown for facilitating his release. All over the world, politicians and everyday citizens asked how and why.

On the day al-Megrahi was released, Annie posted three pictures of her young daughter on Facebook, with the words: "A study in empathy, compassion and sympathy, and an effort to find it in all of its simplicity."

Al-Megrahi lived for another two years and nine months in a luxury villa with his family, funded by the Libyan government. He even outlived his boss, Muammar Qaddafi.

✛

Al-Megrahi's release finally pushed me to write the article I'd promised Annie a year earlier. The article was published online and edited for length and a certain sharpness that journalism often requires. But it didn't tell Annie's whole story. And it certainly didn't answer the questions, *my* questions, about what it means to survive. So, I kept writing, but this time through fiction. I wrote a short story about a woman who'd lost friends to a terrorist attack twenty years earlier, and meets a man who brings it all back. But at some point, I was no longer writing Annie's story. I was writing mine.

From the first moment Annie said those words to me—all my friends were on it—I'd wondered how someone survives loss. Six years after that winter night, I lost my mom. Twenty-two years later, my dad died, and the next year, my brother. In between were aunts and uncles and friends—goddamn, my friends—whose lives were cut short. I didn't lose them to a massive terrorist attack, but I did have to grapple with the question of how to survive.

And here's the answer: I survived imperfectly. Sloppily. Unheroically. With therapy and suicide ideation and antidepressants and sometimes unbearable pain, and a husband who anchored me to something beyond my pain, beyond my loss. To love. I continue to survive by putting a voice to my loss. I don't believe grief can be controlled or eliminated, not even by art. But it can be given a shape, a structure, something to pour itself into.

My grief is my story, and the bombing is Annie's. Sometime around 2013, I apologized for co-opting her story. We were sitting in a mostly deserted coffee shop in Portland, and by that time Annie's dad had died, too. We were both orphans. "Untethered," was the word we both used. I never meant to take something from her, I said. Annie waved her long, thin hand and told me it was okay. It wasn't just her story, she said. She'd released it to the world.

In 2019, Annie flew to Lockerbie, to the memorial built for her friends and the other victims. She talked with people who'd been there, on the ground, who'd sorted through the crash debris. And she wrote. She is still writing. She is putting a voice to her loss. The story of the bombing and how she survived belongs to her, and the story of my family and how I survived belongs to me. And the place where those stories crisscross is the story of us all.

BIBLIOGRAPHY

General

Gordon, Robert J. *The Rise and Fall of American Growth: The U.S. Standard of Living Since the Civil War*. Princeton University Press, 2016.

Howe, Neil & Bill Strauss. *13th Gen: Abort, Retry, Ignore, Fail?* Vintage Books, 1993.

Howe, Neil & Bill Strauss. *The Fourth Turning: What the Cycles of History Tell Us About America's Next Rendezvous with Destiny*. Broadway Books, 1997.

Novak, Dr. Jill. "The Six Living Generations In America." *Marketing Teacher*, https://www.marketingteacher.com/the-six-living-generations-in-america/.

The Indian Way

American Experience. "Native Americans and Mount Rushmore." *PBS*, https://www.pbs.org/wgbh/americanexperience/features/rushmore-sioux/.

Apted, Michael, director. *Thunderheart*. Tristar Pictures, 1992.

Asmelash, Leah. "Native Tribal Leaders Are Calling for the Removal of Mount Rushmore." *CNN*. July 2, 2020. https://www.cnn.com/2020/07/02/us/cheyenne-river-sioux-tribe-mount-rushmore-trnd/.

Brown, Dee. *Bury My Heart at Wounded Knee*. Open Road Media. October 23, 2012.

Chertoff, Emily. "Occupy Wounded Knee: A 71-Day Siege and a Forgotten Civil Rights Movement." *The Atlantic*. October 23, 2012. https://www.theatlantic.com/national/archive/2012/10/occupy-wounded-knee-a-71-day-siege-and-a-forgotten-civil-rights-movement/263998/.

Corbett, Ben. "Caged Warrior: interviews Leonard Peltier." Originally appeared in *Boulder Weekly*, March 13, 2000. Now at http://www.dickshovel.com/AIMIntro.html.

Foderaro, Lisa W. "Richard Wilson, 55, Tribal Head In Occupation of Wounded Knee." Obituaries, *New York Times,* Feb. 4, 1990. https://www.nytimes.com/1990/02/04/obituaries/richard-wilson-55-tribal-head-in-occupation-of-wounded-knee.html.

Friends of Pine Ridge. https://friendsofpineridgereservation.org.

Hoffmeyer, Liz. "American Indian Powwows: Multiplicity and Authenticity." *Smithsonian Center for Folklife & Cultural Heritage.* https://folklife.si.edu/online-exhibitions/american-indian-powwows/Smithsonian.

O'Dowd, Peter and Samantha Raphelson. "50 Years After Mount Rushmore Occupation, Native Americans Are Still Fighting." WBUR, July 3, 2020. https://www.wbur.org/hereandnow/2020/07/03/native-americans-mount-rushmore-protest.

Trimble, Charles E. "Honor the Goons? Never!" *Indian Country Today,* Apr 21, 2004.

Way, Ron. "The Real History of Mount Rushmore: A tourist mecca cut from stone and a sinister delusion of destiny." *Star Tribune,* July 29, 2016. https://www.startribune.com/the-real-history-of-mount-rushmore/388715411/.

Reckoning

"Christine Blasey Ford's Opening Statement For Senate Hearing." *NPR,* September 26, 2018. https://www.npr.org/2018/09/26/651941113/read-christine-blasey-fords-opening-statement-for-senate-hearing.

Maass, Brian. "No Criminal Charges, But 3 Kent Students Not Coming Back." *4CBS Denver,* June 7, 2012. https://denver.cbslocal.com/2012/06/07/no-criminal-charges-but-3-kent-students-not-coming-back/.

Roberts, Michael. "Kent Denver Students Under Investigation for Vail Sex Assault." *Westword,* February 9, 2012. https://www.westword.com/news/kent-denver-students-under-investigation-for-vail-sex-assault-5847773.

Sweet, Ellen. "Date Rape Revisited." *Women's Media Center*, February 23, 2012. https://www.womensmediacenter.com/news-features/date-rape-revisited.

Culture Shock

Bunyak Research Associates. "Denver Area Post-World War II Suburbs." *Front Range Research Associates, Inc.*, April 2011. https://www.codot.gov/programs/research/pdfs/2011/suburbs.pdf.

Carpenter, Faedra Chatard. "Addressing The Complexities of Skin Color: Intra-Racism and the Plays of Hurston, Kennedy, and Orlandersmith. " In *Theatre Topics*. Johns Hopkins University Press, Volume 19, Number 1. March 2009,15-27. https://muse.jhu.edu/article/260771/pdf.

Cherland, Summer Marie. "No Prejudice Here: Racism, Resistance, and the Struggle for Equality in Denver, 1947-1994." 2014. UNLV Theses, Dissertations, Professional Papers, and Capstones. 2526. http://dx.doi.org/10.34917/8220094.

Cole, B. Erin. "R-O: Race, Sexuality and Single-Family Zoning in Denver's Park Hill and Capitol Hill Neighborhoods, 1956-1989." University of New Mexico, Department of History. 2014. https://digitalrepository.unm.edu/hist_etds/14.

Denver Public Library. Five Points-Whittier Neighborhood History, Genealogy, African American & Western History Resources. https://history.denverlibrary.org/five-points-whittier-neighborhood-history.

Graland Country Day: About Us. https://www.graland.org/about-us.

Jones, Trina. "Shades of Brown: The Law of Skin Color." *Duke Law Journal*, vol. 49, 1487-1557. https://scholarship.law.duke.edu/cgi/viewcontent.cgi?article=1052&context=faculty_scholarship.

Ware, Leland. "Color Struck: Intragroup and Cross-racial Color Discriminations." *Public Interest Law Journal*, Fall-Winter 2013, 75-119.

A Letter to Frederick Lyman

Abelson, Jenn, Bella English, Jonathan Saltzman, Todd Wallack, with editors Scott Allen and Amanda Katz. "Private schools, painful secrets," *Boston Globe*. May 6, 2016. https://www. bostonglobe.com/metro/2016/05/06/private-schools-painful-secrets/ OaRI9PFpRnCTJxCzko5hkN/story.html.

Anderson, Travis. "Prep School Finds Five Cases of Sexual Misconduct." *Boston Globe*, August 30, 2016. https://www.bostonglobe.com/ metro/2016/08/30/andover-prep-school-says-three-former-teachers-committed-sexual-misconduct-and/Msz7MDHCNAtKaJj6hvoWxK/ story.html.

Dangremond, Sam. "Andover Sex Abuse Report Includes a Teacher Also Named By Choate." *Town & Country Magazine*, August 1, 2017. https:// www.townandcountrymag.com/society/a10398813/phillips-andover-sex-abuse-report/.

Globe Staff. "Understanding the sexual abuse allegations at New England prep schools." *Boston Globe*, July 23, 2016. https://www.bostonglobe.com/ news/special-reports/2016/07/23/understanding-sexual-abuse-allegations-new-england-prep-schools/on22ht2ORzSB9Z2Prz5v0O/story.html.

Harris, Elizabeth A., "In a Brief Prep School Career, a Growing List of Sexual Misconduct Allegations." *New York Times*, June 1, 2017. https:// www.nytimes.com/2017/06/01/nyregion/choate-frederic-lyman-sexual-misconduct-allegations.html.

Harris, Elizabeth A. "Love, Rick: Teacher's Letters Track an Attempted Seduction." *New York Times*, May 25, 2017. https://www.nytimes. com/2017/05/25/nyregion/choate-school-sex-abuse-letters.html.

Harris, Elizabeth A. "Ousted Over Sexual Misconduct Claims, and On to the Next Teaching Job." *New York Times*, April 23, 2017. https://www. nytimes.com/2017/04/23/nyregion/ousted-over-sexual-misconduct-claims-and-on-to-the-next-teaching-job.html.

Harris, Elizabeth A. "Third School Report Finds Sexual Misconduct by Choate Teacher." *New York Times,* August 1, 2017. https://www.nytimes.com/2017/08/01/nyregion/third-school-report-finds-sexual-misconduct-by-choate-teacher.html.

Kestenbaum, Nancy. "Report to the Board of Trustees of Choate Rosemary Hall," Covington & Burling LLP, April 2017.

"Prestigious Prep School Facing Additional Sexual Abuse Charges." *New York Post* via *Associated Press,* August 1, 2017. https://nypost.com/2017/08/01/prestigious-prep-school-facing-additional-sexual-abuse-charges/.

Scenes From My Youth

Avildsen, John G., director. *Rocky.* Chartoff-Winkler Productions, 1976. Distributed by United Artists.

Hughes, John, director. *Sixteen Candles.* Universal Pictures, 1984.

Hursley, Doris, Frank Hursley, Patricia Falken Smith, and Carey Wilber, writers. *General Hospital.* Directed by Phil Sogard. Aired October 4, 1979. ABC.

Reitman, Ivan, director. *Meatballs.* Dunning/Link/Reitman Productions, 1979. Distributed in the USA by Paramount Pictures.

Schumacher, Joel, director. *St. Elmo's Fire.* Columbia Pictures, 1985.

That Long Weird Essay That's Entirely About Beverly Hills 90210

Itzkoff, Dave. "When Teenage Angst Had Its Own ZIP Code." *New York Times,* August 29, 2008. https://www.nytimes.com/2008/08/31/arts/television/31itzk.html.

Lippman, John. "Fox Network Gets Cable Affiliates in Deal With TCI." *Los Angeles Times,* September 7, 1990. https://www.latimes.com/archives/la-xpm-1990-09-07-fi-566-story.html.

Meltzer, Marisa. "When Brenda Walsh Was Young: The Revolutionary First Season of Beverly Hills, 90210." Slate, December 7, 2006. https://slate.com/culture/2006/12/the-revolutionary-first-season-of-beverly-hills-90210.html.

Star, Darren, creator. *Beverly Hills, 90210.* Numerous episodes and writers, seasons 1-10. Spelling Television, 1990-2000.

Stauth, Cameron. "Fox in The Network Henhouse." *New York Times*, July 15, 1990. https://www.nytimes.com/1990/08/19/magazine/l-fox-in-the-network-henhouse-509390.html.

Magnum Force

Carrns, Ann. "Reverse Mortgage Lenders Fined for Ads That 'Tricked' Older Borrowers." *New York Times*, Dec. 9, 2016. https://www.nytimes.com/2016/12/09/your-money/reverse-mortgage-lenders-fined-for-ads-that-tricked-older-borrowers.html.

Clow, Chris. "AAG Unveils New Selleck Ad to Set Reverse Mortgage Record Straight." *Reverse Mortgage Daily,* July 16, 2019. https://reversemortgagedaily.com/2019/07/16/aag-unveils-new-selleck-ad-to-set-reverse-mortgage-record-straight/.

Consumer Financial Protection Bureau. "CFPB Takes Action Against Reverse Mortgage Companies for Deceptive Advertising." December 07, 2016. https://www.consumerfinance.gov/about-us/newsroom/cfpb-takes-action-against-reverse-mortgage-companies-deceptive-advertising/.

Kaufman, Joanne. "Would You Trust Tom Selleck With Your Life Savings?" *New York Times*, June 23, 2017. https://www.nytimes.com/2017/06/23/business/would-you-trust-tom-selleck-with-your-life-savings.html.

McKim, Jennifer. "More Seniors Are Taking Loans Against Their Homes—And It's Costing Them." *Washington Post*, August 25, 2017. https://www.washingtonpost.com/business/economy/more-seniors-are-taking-loans-against-their-homes--and-its-costing-them/2017/08/25/5f154072-883a-11e7-961d-2f373b3977ee_story.html.

Penzenstadler, Nick, and Jeff Kelly Lowenstein. "Seniors Were Sold a Risk-Free Retirement with Reverse Mortgages. Now They Face Foreclosure." *USA Today*, June 11, 2019. https://www.usatoday.com/in-depth/news/investigations/2019/06/11/seniors-face-foreclosure-retirement-after-failed-reverse-mortgage/1329043001/.

"Tom Selleck Named American Advisors Group (AAG) National Spokesman." *Business Wire*, June 01, 2016. https://www.businesswire.com/news/home/20160601006928/en/Tom-Selleck-Named-American-Advisors-Group-AAG-National-Spokesman.

Young, Roger, director. *Magnum, P.I.* Season 1, episodes 1 & 2. "Don't Eat the Snow in Hawaii." Universal Television, aired CBS December 11, 1980.

Blood Brothers

Boyle, Mary. "Denver Shaken By Rash Of Crime By Skinheads." *Washington Post*, November 22, 1997. https://www.washingtonpost.com/archive/politics/1997/11/22/denver-shaken-by-rash-of-crime-by-skinheads/0b63a57d-cd98-49fd-bbdf-900b815fe78d/.

Brooke, James. "From Close Family to World of Hate." *New York Times*, December 13, 1997. https://www.nytimes.com/1997/12/13/us/from-close-family-to-world-of-hate.html.

Carman, Diane. "Juror: We got sucked in," *Denver Post*, May 2, 2000. https://extras.denverpost.com/news/lisl0502.htm.

Carman, Diane. "Lisl Auman: Hostage or Accomplice?" *Denver Post*. April 30, 2000. https://extras.denverpost.com/news/lisl0430.htm.

Locker, Melissa. "Vanity Fair Confidential Goes Deep on True Crime in New TV Show." *Vanity Fair*, January 19, 2015. https://www.vanityfair.com/hollywood/2015/01/vanity-fair-confidential-id-tv.

Murr, Andrew. "Didn't Seem Like Much." *Newsweek*, November 30, 1997. https://www.newsweek.com/didnt-seem-much-170940.

Officer Down Memorial Page: Police Officer Bruce VanderJagt. https://www.odmp.org/officer/15002-police-officer-bruce-vanderjagt.

Seal, Mark. "Prisoner of Denver." *Vanity Fair,* June 2004. https://www.vanityfair.com/news/2004/06/innocent-murderer-200406.

Turf, Luke. "Suns Set." *Westword,* December 15, 2005. https://www.westword.com/news/suns-set-5087761.

"Vanity Fair Confidential: Prisoner of Denver." Investigation Discovery Channel, Season 1, ep. 3. 2015. Conde Nest Entertainment.

Wittman, Juliet. "From Kid to Killer." (an alternate version titled "Zero to Life" also appeared) *Westword,* April 15, 1999. https://www.westword.com/news/from-kid-to-killer-5059767.

Falling Off Radar

Cowell, Alan, and A. G. Sulzberger. "Lockerbie Convict Returns to Jubilant Welcome." *New York Times,* Aug. 21, 2009. https://archive.nytimes.com/www.nytimes.com/learning/students/pop/articles/21lockerbie.html.

"Pan Am Bombing." FBI History: Famous Cases & Criminals. https://www.fbi.gov/history/famous-cases/pan-am-103-bombing.

"Pan Am Flight 103." Lockerbie Air Disaster Archives, Syracuse University. https://panam103.syr.edu.

"When Pan Am Flight 103 Exploded Over Lockerbie, Scotland on December 21, 1988, it Was Carrying 35 Syracuse University Students Home from A Semester Spent Studying Abroad." https://www.syracuse.edu/about/history/pan-am-103-remembrance/.

Whitney, Craig R. "Jetliner Carrying 258 To U.S. Crashes In Scottish Town." *New York Times,* Dec. 22, 1988. https://www.nytimes.com/1988/12/22/world/jetliner-carrying-258-to-us-crashes-in-scottish-town.html.

Publishing Acknowledgements

Thank you to the following publications for originally publishing these essays:

"A Letter to Frederic Lyman and the Plethora of Other Private School Teachers Who Sexually Abused Their Students," *Harpur Palate*, Issue 21

"Scenes From My Youth," *Entropy*

"Long and Thin," *Berkeley Fiction Review*, in a slightly different form

"Blood Brothers," *River Teeth*

"Flights of Two," *Sport Literate*

"Falling Off Radar," *Salon*, in a slightly different form, with the title "The Flight She Missed"

To the Totally Rad & Righteous

I knew Andrew Gifford at SFWP was the perfect publisher for these essays when he said he understood the dangers of nostalgia. Thank you, Andrew for wanting this book so much.

Victor Chayet was foundational to this project, with his brilliant insights, thoughtful conversations, clever jokes, and support to keep on keeping-on. I love you, sir.

Mad love to my small press sister, Wendy Fox. To Yuvi Zalkow, Jackie Shannon Hollis, and Scott Sparling for their unwavering camaraderie and writerly help. Mahalo to Pat McDonald for giving insight and direction on the manuscript when I was wondering, "Is this a thing?" Karen Karbo and Aaron Gilbreath also helped steer the ship in the right direction. Laura Stanfill: I've said it before and I'll say it again, it means everything that you like and love me for who I am.

I'm eternally grateful to the people who shared their stories, and helped my heart grow and understand experiences outside my own. Many of these resilient souls chose to remain anonymous, so I'll just say: You know who you are, and you are beautiful. I have nothing but awe-filled respect for the bravery of the former students who spoke their truth: Christine Blasey Ford, Cheyenne Montgomery, Jane Marion, and all the other women and men who contributed to the investigations into abuse at private schools.

Big-ass appreciation to Nicole Schmidt, my sharp and funny editor: Girl, if/when we see each other IRL, you're getting a gigantic hug and some silly tropical drink (possibly in a whole pineapple. Okay, it'll definitely be in a whole pineapple).

It took me decades to appreciate my rarified high school experience, with the good and the bad living side-by-side. Kent Denver: thank you for El Pomar and the amphitheater and the lower lake and the commons room, and for all the dedicated teachers. Keep moving forward in your work to understand and address racial and gender inequalities. I'm proud to be an alum.

Major love and mondo gratitude to my totally awesome, tubular husband, Michael. Like, fer sure, you know?

About the Author

Liz Prato is the author of *Volcanoes, Palm Trees, and Privilege: Essays on Hawai'i*, a 2019 New York Times Top Summer Read and Oregon Book Award Finalist; the short story collection *Baby's on Fire*; and editor of *The Night, and the Rain, and the River*. Liz grew up in Denver and now lives in Portland, Oregon with her best friend/husband, who is a bookseller, musician, and writer. She lives for small presses, indie bookstores, community, and palm trees.

More essays from Santa Fe Writers Project

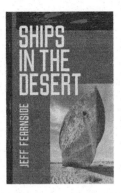

Ships in the Desert by *Jeff Fearnside*

Ships in the Desert takes us to Kazakhstan and explores universal issues of religious bigotry, cultural intolerance, environmental degradation, and how a battle over water rights led to a catastrophe that is now being repeated around the world.

"Fearnside helps make clear what is to so many in the West a little known and mysterious part of our world."

— Kurt Caswell, author of Laika's Window: The Legacy of a Soviet Space Dog

The Dangerous Joy of Dr. Sex
by *Pagan Kennedy*

Join Pagan Kennedy as she explores the true story behind *The Joy of Sex*, visits visits with a retired chemist who is trying to turn a wasteland into paradise, interviews an aspiring tyrant who wishes to become the emperor of America, and becomes a test subject for an artist who has created a "brain machine" made from parts he bought at Radio Shack.

"A dangerous joy of literary pleasure—a compelling, spellbinding reading experience"

— Lee Gutkind, author of Almost Human: Making Robots Think

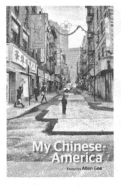

My Chinese-America by *Allen Gee*

This not-to-be-missed collection from SFWP Awards Program winner Gee has an intimacy that transcends cultural boundaries, and casts light on a vital part of American culture that surrounds and influences all of us.

"Masculinity, mobility, history, and the American dream of equality all take their turn under Gee's lens, as he shrewdly navigates a culture saturated with the privilege of white America and the realities of continued segregation in the so-called New South."

— Publishers Weekly

About Santa Fe Writers Project

SFWP is an independent press founded in 1998. We publish exciting fiction and creative nonfiction of every genre.

 @santafewritersproject | @SFWP | www.sfwp.com